Cover Your Head

A Pictographic Chronicle of the Moslem Turban

Edited, Illustrated, Arranged by
Sis. Tauheedah S. Najee-Ullah El

Compiled by
G.S., D.M. Bro. Kudjo Adwo El

(C)over Your Head
A Pictographic Chronicle of the Moslem Turban

© 2022 Califa Media Publishing*
A Moorish Guide Publishing Company

Edited, Illustrated, & Arranged by
Sis. Tauheedah S. Najee-Ullah El
Califa Media Publishing

Compiled by
G.S., D.M. Bro. Kudjo Adwo El
M.S.T.A. Subordinate Temple #5 - Canaanland

ISBNs:
Hardcover - 978-1-952828-22-5
Paperback - 978-1-952828-23-2 (Color)
Paperback - 978-1-952828-25-6 (Black & White)
Electronic - 978-1-952828-24-9

Library of Congress Control # 2022951539

All Rights Reserved. Without Prejudice. No Part Of This Book May Be Reproduced Or Transmitted In Any Form By Any Means, Electronic, Photocopying, Mechanical, Recording, Information Storage Or Retrieval System Unless For The Liberation Of Minds And Gaining Knowledge Of Self.

CalifaMedia.com

*Califa Media Publishing is a d.b.a. of MOORISH RELIGIOUS & CULTURAL INSTITUTE INC.
Cover Design by Sis. T. S. Najee-Ullah El

Contents

MOORISH AMERICAN PRAYER	I.
EDITOR'S NOTE	II.
MEMORANDUM & INTRODUCTION	III.
ACKNOWLEDGEMENT & THANKS	IV.
CHAPTER 1 Defining the Turban	1
CHAPTER 2 India	11
CHAPTER 3 Europe	21
CHAPTER 4 Africa America	69
CHAPTER 5 Noble Drew Ali's Holy Crown	83
CHAPTER 6 Wrapping the Moorish Turban	87
REFERENCES	97
OTHER WORKS FROM **CALIFA MEDIA PUBLISHING**	105

Moorish American Prayer

·····

Allah

Father of the Universe, the Father
of Love, Truth, Peace, Freedom and Justice. ALLAH
is my Protection, my Guide and my Salvation By Night
and by Day, through Her Holy Prophet Noble Drew Ali.

·····

AMEN

Editor's Note

Islam, and Greetings. Gratitude for your interest in Moorish Moslem history and willingness to receive it from a Moorish perspective. This, and all of Califa Media's publications, remind me of a the statement (warning?) by Dr. Donald Fixico of the importance of a people telling their own story. Dr. Fixico has the distinction of being the first Native American to earn a PhD in History and I am profoundly honored to have been able to sit in his class and hear historic details never mentioned during my free "education."

The reader is encouraged to have close at a good, standard dictionary of the English language, preferably one printed before 1965. I suggest using a dictionary of this sort as many definitions—especially those pertaining to our people—were altered after the Civil Rights Movement in the United States. An example would be comparing the definitions of "American" in a pre-1965 dictionary versus one printed more recently. There is no glossary contained in this text to encourage use of a dictionary. Man—nor woman— knows not by being told. It should be further noted that this book was written in the interest of the persistent scholar, and this is reflected in vocabulary.

Please note that this text poses questions alongside researched information. The reason for this is two-fold: first to challenge the "facts" and suppositions of those who benefit from our continued lack of self-knowledge. Second, to encourage (push?) the Moorish reader to fill in those blanks.

Also please note that the majority of the images contained in this text fall within the category of creative common / public domain works. Those that may not be classified as such have been used in good faith for the purpose of education and edification pursuant to the Fair Use Clause of the SS 107 of the U.S. Copyright Act. Gratitude to those creators and trustees of the herein contained works for their contribution to the activation of the genetic memory banks of Moorish Americans Moslems.

Peace & Love
Sis. Tauheedah S. Najee-Ullah El
Managing Editor - Califa Media Publishing

Acknowledgments & Thanks

Contributors to this work include, but are not limited to:

Sis. RahsMariah Bey
Bro. G.S. Aatazaz Bey
Bro. Kasir Effie Raj El
Sis. Noble Sunny Bey
Bro. Aseer El

Gratitude to those creators and trustees of the herein contained works for their contribution to the genetic memory bank re-activation of Moorish Americans Moslems.

Memorandum & Introduction

Pictographic:
  A pictorial representation of numerical data or relationships, especially a graph, but having each value represented by a proportional number of pictures.[1]

Chronicle:
  A "chronicle" is a chronological visual record of an event, person, or thing, with photos from one person, or many.[2]

Per the above definitions, the numerical values are the dates of production for the related items contained herein, demonstrating the evolution of the turban not only over time, but providing evidence just how far back Moors are recoded in the annals of history.

The layout of the book is designed to invoke the impression of strolling through a museum or an art gallery, with images being arranged according to [continental] location then chronologically.

Key 44: Where did Jesus Teach?
India, Africa, and Europe[3]

While the turban has been represented across continents and over ages, for the sake of brevity, this text will focus on locations graced by the presence of Jesus during his lifetime. According to the teachings of the Prophet Noble Drew Ali, lands known today as America (A-Mooroco) were the shores of Northwest and Southwest Africa until they were separated by the great cataclysm that resulted in the formation of the Atlantic Ocean. In that light, the sections on Africa and America are presented as a single entity.

---

  1. "Pictographic," The Free Dictionary (Farlex), accessed August 20, 2022, https://www.thefreedictionary.com/pictographic.

  2. "What Is a 'Chronicle'?," Chronicle, accessed August 20, 2022, https://www.onechronicle.com/help/.

  3. Timothy Noble Drew Ali, "Koran Questions for Moorish Americans: 101s and Additional Laws," in *Califa Uhuru: A Compilation of Literature from the Moorish Science Temple of America*, ed. Tauheedah Najee-Ullah El, vol. 4 (Lafayette, Indiana: Califa Media Publishing, 2014), 138-148.

Chapter 1

Defining the Turban
Makes, Models, & Metaphysics

The turban is the highest diadem of the Moslem. While it's exact origins remain unclear, an early example of the turban can be found on a royal Mesopotamian sculpture dated circa 2350. For millennia, the turban has been worn to indicate the wearer's connection to the highest levels of scholarship, nobility, or divinity upon sight. When referring to Moorish Moslems, it usually meant a combination of these three. This unmistakable sign of Moslem influence has spanned the globe, becoming one of the most enduring symbols of our presence. While the style, adornments, and wearer changed with location and time, common themes remained.

Physical and Health Benefits

There are 26 bones in the human skull. Wrapping turban compresses all of these bones together, giving the wearer a sense of stability and clarity. The covering of the temples is a means of preventing the thoughts of others from entering the mind.

In Sikh tradition, it is said the soft spot at the top of an infants head is the opening to the 10th gate, also known as the Crown chakra. This practice teaches that the hair covering this gate protects it from the elements while simultaneously acting as an antenna. To increase the effect of this antenna, Sikh tie the hair into a *joora* coil, known traditionally as a *rishi* knot, a *rishi* being someone able to channel pranic or spiritual energy. Adding turban to this process activates pressure centers in the skull, invoking a sense of calm and increasing blood flow to the brain.

Many wear the turban to protect their antenna (hair), however they don't necessarily wrap with the cross above the brow. The cross ought not be omitted is because it creates the triune symbol and accentuates the pineal. When you wrap a turban upon your head, it is a divine occurrence.

A Rose by Many Other Names

Early references to the word *turban* reveal it's modern name derives from the ancient Persian word *dhulban*, meaning rose-petal. This is owning to the folds of the turban and their resemblance to rose petals, with roses metaphycically representing the love of Allah for man.[1,2] As the turban migrated with their owners across time and space, its name changes reveal clues as to how its association was adjusted to the wearers new circumstances. The following is a short list gathered from Spanish fashion history and their translations:[3]

Alamaizar/ Almaysar
Arabic: Shrine, For Shrine.

Toca, Tocas
Spanish: Touch, Feel, Sense, Press.

Tocas Tunesies
(Tocas) Spanish: Touch, Feel, Sense, Press

(Tunecies) Spanish: Tunisia,

Tocas de Camino
(Tocas) Spanish: Touch, Feel, Sense, Press

(Camino) Spanish: Way, Road, Path, Journey

Alhareme/ Alfareme/ Alfileme
Spanish: the harem.

> *"The voluminous folds of the turban— called in Morocco rozzah or 'amarah— though a trifle irritating to the novice, are a splendid shield from the sun, and altogether there is much more to be said in favour of this head-gear than of that crowning barbarity of civilization, the 'top hat' or 'stove-pipe.'"*[4]

---

1. Leon Saul, "The History of the Turban," *UPrising International*, February 2010, Vol 16 #10 edition.

2. Tiara Dennis, "Rose Symbolism: New Beginning and Hope," Sun Signs, July 14, 2021, https://www.sunsigns.org/rose-symbolism-meanings/.

3. Consuelo, "La Toca, Turbantes (Y Ii)," LA TOCA, Turbantes (y II), January 1, 1970, https://opusincertumhispanicus.blogspot.com/2013/02/la-toca-y-2.html.

4. Budgett Meakin, "How the Moors Dress," in *The Moors: A Comprehensive Description* (London, 1906), 58.

Adornments

Cloth

During the Moorish occupation of Al Andalus, turban were generally wrapped in linen, as prescribed by the Abrahamic religions. The white cloth, likely linen, is seen repeated in paintings and drawings of the indigenous Moors first encountered by modern European colonists. Other cloth choices included hollandaise, chiffon, foam, and silk. The most expensive turbans were wrapped silk covered in displays of the wearer's wealth and/ or prestige.

Highly adorned turban were known as toca Morisca, or Moorish toca, and were worn primarily during special occasions due to their opulence.[5] Natural, breathable fibers, are preferable, especially when using more cloth to wrap larger turban.

Feathers

Across time and culture, the feather has symbolized a connection to spirituality. One of the earliest examples of feather iconography is found in ancient Egypt, where the goddess Ma'at had as her symbol a single ostrich feather. This Feather of Truth serves as a symbol of her higher principles, personified truth, morality, order and justice—the principles that guided the life of every Egyptian. The ancient Druids are said to have attached feathers to their robes for rites and ceremonies where they wanted to connect to sky gods and access spiritual knowledge.[6] In early Christianity, the peacock feather represented the resurrection of Christ, as the peacock regrows it's feathers each year, and were used as reminders of the soul's everlasting life. They have also been

---

5. Consuelo.

6. K. M. Sheard, *Llewellyn's Complete Book of Names: For Pagans, Witches, Wiccans, Druids, Heathens, Mages, Shamans and Independent Thinkers of All Sorts Who Are Curious About Names from Every Place and Every Time* (Minneapolis, MN: Llewellyn, 2012).

Musicians in Havana, Cuba, 1860.

used to remind Christians of the virtues of faith, hope, and faith.[7]

Perhaps the most well known use of feathers in headdress is that of th indigenous Americans. Among most of these tribes and nations, it is still traditional to give feathers as signs of respect, courage, or strength. The bird species, the feather color, size, number, even the area of the body harvested from further indicated the wearers status, and even feats accomplished.[8,9]

Bird	Feather Meaning[10]
Dove	holy spirit, promise of new life, peace, purity
Eagle	dignity, honor, pride, protection, renewal, strength
Hawk	clarity, decisiveness, foresight, physical health, strength
Heron	balance, self-reliance, stability, tact, wisdom
Ostrich	afterlife, judgment, sin, truth,
Owl	bad omens, wisdom, death
Peacock	leadership, peace, self-discovery, regeneration
Pheasant	agility, swift change, transitions
Raven	intelligence, insight, loyalty, protection, transformation
Rooster	aggression, fearlessness, masculinity, virility
Swan	harmony, loyalty, purity
Turkey	abundance, fertility, pride

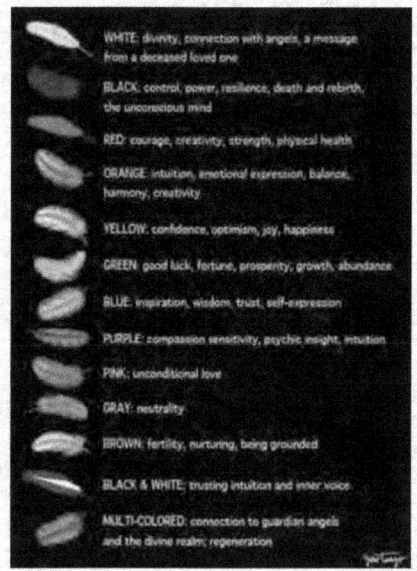

---

7. Carol Holaday, *Crafting a Magical Life: Manifesting Your Heart's Desire Through Creative Projects* (Forres, Scotland: Findhorn Press, 2009).

8. Jack Tresidder, "Feather," in *The Watkins Dictionary of Symbols* (London: Watkins, 2008).

9. "The Spiritual Meaning & Symbolism of Feathers," YourTango, July 4, 2022, https://www.yourtango.com/2020337386/feather-meanings-spiritual-meaning-symbolism-feathers.

10. "Feather Meaning and Spiritual Symbolism: The Ultimate Guide," A Little Spark of Joy, May 8, 2022, https://www.alittlesparkofjoy.com/feather-meaning/.

Gemstones

Ancient Hindu cosmology illustrates how gemstones have been connected symbolically with planets, days of the week and deities. As with most things in life, the effects of some stones were beneficial while others were detrimental. Beneficial stones included diamonds, pearls, emeralds, and topaz. Stones thought to carry malefic energies include cat's eye, coral, sapphire, and ruby.[11] Of highest esteem is an ornament known as a *navaratna* that contains one stone for each of the "nine celestial deities."[12] It is thought that the stones acts as a seat for the associated deity, inviting them to intercede on the wearer's behalf. Tradition describes the order of the stones as placing the ruby (Sun) at the center of the arranged stones, followed clockwise from the top: diamond, pearl, red coral, hessonite, blue sapphire, cat's eye, yellow sapphire, and emerald.[13]

A Navaratna turban with nine sacred gemstones. C. Krishniah Chetty and Sons

Deity	Planet	Sign	Stone/ Gem	Power
Surya	Sun	Leo	Ruby	energy, power, prestige, fame
Shukra	Venus	Taurus, Libra	Diamond	riches, power, marital bliss
Chandra	Moon	Cancer	Pearl	peace, emotional stability, creativity
Mangala	Mars	Aries, Scorpio	Red Coral	physical strength, beauty, happy marriage, agility
Rahu	Moon's North Node	N/A	Hessonite	legal & political success
Shani	Saturn	Capricorn, Aquarius	Blue Sapphire	protection, status, cure depression, wards off evil eyes
Ketu	Moon's South Node	N/A	Cat's Eye	protects from scandal, hidden enemies, scandal
Guru	Jupiter	Sagittarius, Pisces	Yellow Sapphire	luck, prosperity, wisdom, judgment, wealth
Budha	Mercury	Gemini, Virgo	Emerald	concentration, mental clarity, intellectual power

---

11. Courtney A. Stewart, "In the Stars: Gems and the Indian Tradition," Metmuseum.org, December 17, 2014, https://www.metmuseum.org/blogs/now-at-the-met/2014/in-the-stars-gems-and-the-indian-tradition.

12. Sunny Diamonds, "Everything You Should Know About Navaratna Diamond Jewellery," Sunny Diamonds, June 21, 2021, https://sunnydiamonds.com/blog/everything-you-should-know-about-navaratna-diamond-jewellery.

13. Abhilash MS, "Traditional Settings of Navaratna Gems," Traditional Settings of Navaratna Gems (Hindu Devotional Blog, July 6, 2021), https://www.hindudevotionalblog.com/2011/12/traditional-settings-of-navaratna-gems.html.

Colors

As the name and form of the turban changed over time and location, the associated colors followed suit. Along with the size, shape and cloth, a turban's color can still be used not only reveal one's status at a glance, but indicate one's allegiance, profession, and even task for that day. During the reign of the Moors in Sicily, a soldier loyal to the Abbasid caliphate was immediately recognized by his domed helmet wrapped in a black turban.[14] In cosmopolitan Ottoman Istanbul, turban color was used to indicate religious affiliation, with Jews wearing yellow, Christians in blue, Zoroastrians in black, and only Turks in white.[15] In areas of Rajastan, arrangement of colors in specific patterns can reveal one's social status, wealth, lineage, and/ or ceremony being attended.[16] Today, contemporary Moorish Moslems can be found wearing the turban in the color corresponding to the day of the week or business being attended to. Some common metaphysical meanings of colors in most cultures today:[17]

Color	Meaning
Red	ambition, anger, blood, passion, will, wine
Orange	adventurous, fire, nurturing
Yellow	the sun, active solar energy, majesty, willpower
Green	vegetation, growth, fertility, good fortune;,
Blue	earth, justice, peace, perseverance, vigilance
Indigo	clairvoyance, dignity, intuition, knowledge
Violet	power, royalty, spirituality
Black	absorption, alchemical prime matter, death, midnight
White	healing, innocence, purity, reflection, ruler of the land
Gold	divinity, durability, enlightenment, power, victory, wisdom

---

14. David Nicolle and Angus McBride, in *The Moors: The Islamic West 7th-15th Century AD* (Oxford: Osprey Military, 2008), 44.

15. Connor H. Richardson, "The Coverings of an Empire: An Examination of Ottoman Headgear from 1500 to 1829," The Cupola: Scholarship at Gettysburg College, 2012, https://cupola.gettysburg.edu/student_scholarship/104, 3.

16. Team Utsav Pedia, "Turban or Pagri: The Pride of Marwar," Utsavpedia, May 2, 2017, https://www.utsavpedia.com/attires/pagri-the-pride-of-marwar/.

17. Mishaal Talib Mahfuz El Bey, *The Torch: A Guide to S.E.L.F.* (Lafayette, Indiana: Califa Media Publishing, 2020), 461.

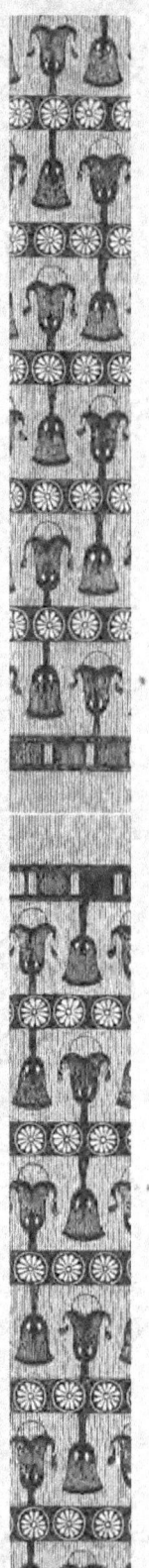

Associations

With the establishment of civilization came the need for stratification to ensure society ran smoothly and efficiently. To aid in this efficiency, it would help to be able to recognize a person's status and rank at a glance, doing away with the need to question a party asserting a certain authority. In times past, these were known as sumptuary laws, and the concept was applied globally in nearly identical ways, with the most extreme version being carried out in feudal Japan. The pecking order is universal amongst humans, and those at "the top" are still insecure that the rabble might dare imitate their "betters." In this section, we look at how the turban has been used in distinguishing the commoner from the individuals of higher status.

Scholarship

The turban is the traditional headdress of Sufi mystics, these scholars often being recognized by their green wraps. In modern media, the turban is synonymous with a fortune teller or someone in possession of mysterious wisdom. The Victorian fascination with Egyptology, spiritualism, mysticism..and magic... and the mysterious nature of the "far east" and eastern mysticism... all these backgrounds helped to make wearing a turban a clear sign that the magician wasn't a skilled trickster but someone with special powers.

> *No one becomes a scholar by virtue of robe and turban.*
> *- Rumi*

Nobility

Turbans have often been worn by nobility, regardless of religion. As shown in Ottoman court depictions, the sultan is immediately recognized in a sea of turbans by his own which was MUCH larger. This royal turban was usually only worn during ceremonies that didn't require physical interaction by the sultan due to its cumbersome size. Though large, it was likely not heavy due to the status of the wearer—research suggests that it consisted of a light-weight balsa wood frame, likely padded for comfort, with only a few layers of actual fabric wrapped around it.[18] This fabric was typically wrapped seven times around the frame. Other depictions show Moors in turban heavily laden in gold and gems, with the highest ranking being marked by additional cloth, jewels, exotic feathers, and other costly adornments.

> For the Mughal rulers of India, the turban and its associated ornaments had the powerful and mystical qualities that crowns had in medieval Europe. The jewels attached to the turban included the kalghi, an aigrete of peacock or heron feathers with a jewel attached to it. This was only conferred on the highest nobles.[19]

Divinity

As shown in numerous graphic depictions of Balthazar and his companions (see *Chapter 3*), divinely appointed people were frequently indicated with the turban. If their royal crowns are shown, it is with the turban wrapped around it, denoting appointment to their position by a higher power than their fellow man. These depictions are supported by the mention of the turban throughout scripture:

> "They made the tunic of fine lines, woven work for Aaron and his sons, the **turban** of fine linen, the tall head dress and their bands all of fine linen, the drawers of finely woven linen, the sash of woven linen, as the Lord had commanded Moses." (Exodus 39:27)

> "These are the vestments they must make: breast plate, ephod, robe, embroidered tunic, **turban** and girdle." (Exodus: 28:4)

> They made a rosette of pure gold as the symbol of their holy dedication and inscribed on it as the engraving on a seal, "Holy to the Lord"; and they fastened it on a violet brand to fix it on the **turban** at the top as the Lord had commanded Moses. (Exodus 39:29)

---

18. Richardson, 5.

19. Bernard S. Cohn, *Colonialism and Its Forms of Knowledge the British in India* (Princeton, NJ: Princeton Univ. Press, 2006), 116.

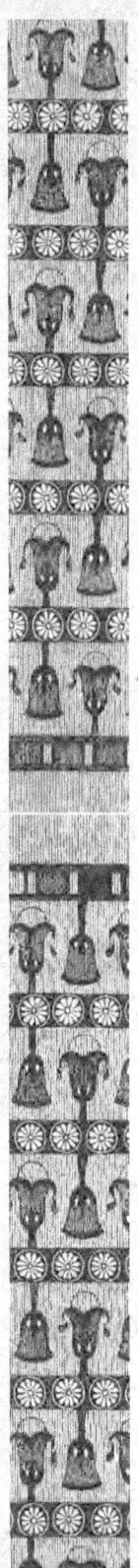

He put the **turban** upon his head and set the gold rosette as symbol of holy dedication on the front of the **turban** as the Lord had commanded him. Moses then took the anointing oil, anointed the Tabernacle and all that was within it and consecrated it. (Leviticus 8:9)

Set the turban on his head and the symbol of holy dedication on the turban. Take the anointing oil, pour it on his head and anoint him. (Exodus 29:6)

They made a rosette of pure gold as the symbol of their holy dedication and inscribed on it as the engraving on a seal, "Holy to the Lord"; and they fastened it on a violet brand to fix it on the **turban** at the top as the Lord had commanded Moses. (Exodus 39:29)

He put the **turban** upon his head and set the gold rosette as symbol of holy dedication on the front of the **turban** as the Lord had commanded him. Moses then took the anointing oil, anointed the Tabernacle and all that was within it and consecrated it. (Leviticus 8:9)

Set the **turban** on his head and the symbol of holy dedication on the **turban**. Take the anointing oil, pour it on his head and anoint him. (Exodus 29:6)

The **turban** and beard gave them such attractive personality that women who had not seen them were infatuated by their personality. No sooner had she seen wall engravings of men, paintings of Chaldeans, colored vermilion, men with sashes round their waists and elaborate **turbans** on their heads, all so imperious of bearing portraits of Babylonians from Chaldea, then she fell in love with them at first sight and sent messengers to them in Chaldea. Belts were round their waists and on their heads, **turbans** with dangling ends; all seemed to be high officers and looked like Babylonian natives of Chaldea. (Ezekiel 23:14-17)

Now Joshua was dressed in dirty clothes as he stood before the angel of God. The angel said these words to those who stood before him: "Take off his dirty clothes, clothe him in splendid robes of state and put a clean **turban** on his head." They clothed him in splendid robes of State and put a clean **turban** on his head. The angel said, "I have taken away your inequity from you. He shall wear a sacred linen tunic and linen drawer to cover himself and he shall put on a linen sash around his waist and wind a linen **turban** round his head and these are sacred vestments and he shall bathe before putting them on." (Zechariah 3:4-9)

She is clothed with neatness, she is fed with temperance; humility and meekness are as a crown of glory circling her head. (Holy Koran MHTS/MSTA Chapter 21)

Chapter 2

India
Khans, Rajas & Sikhs

*Mir Mohammad Khan
Khan of Kalat*

c. 1894

Fred Bremner
British, 1863–1941

Photograph of Sir Mir Mohammad Khan, Khan (ruling chief) of Kalat from the 'Wheeler Collection: Portraits of Indian Rulers,' was taken by Frederick Bremner c.1894. Kalat is located in Baluchistan and was established in the middle of the fifteenth century by the Mir Wari clan, an Arab family."[1]

Arjun Singh
Raja of Narsinghgarh
c. 1900

Herzog & Higgins
British, 19th Century

Photograph of Sir Arjun Singh (1887 - 1924), Raja of Narsinghgarh from the "Wheeler Collection: Portraits of Indian Rulers," taken by Herzog and Higgins c.1900. Born in 1887, Singh was appointed as Raja in 1897 at only ten years of age, gaining full ruling powers from the Government of India in 1909.[2]

Sardar Singh, Maharaja of Jodhpur

c. 1900

Gobindram & Oodeyram
British, 19th Century

*Do not leave me, hide in my heart like a secret,
wind around my head like a turban.*

– Rumi

Maharaj Rameshwar Singhji

Raja of Multhan

c. 1971

Artist Unknown
20th Century

The turban is an inextricable part of the Sikh identity. Sikhs say you may take off their head but not the turban.

– *Preneet Kaur*

Chand Tora Dumalla with many shaster

date unknown

Artist Unknown
21st Century

The Divine Energy that governs the Universe and guides our own life is mostly unknown to us. Living with an awareness of that Divine Energy within oneself and the entire creation allows us to live our highest potential. Wearing the turban helps us experience that Divine Energy and to remember there is something greater than what we know. It is a spiritual practice where we take the highest, most visible part of ourselves and show that it belongs to the Creator. Wearing the turban also helps cultivate a sense of surrender to the Divine.

– Sikh Dharma International

Baba 'Balwant' Singh
2009

Artist Unknown
21st Century

> Baba 'Balwant' Singh, member of the traditional Sikh religious warriors' Nihang Army, poses with his 700 m, 60 kg turban on "Fateh Divas" in Amritsar on October 18, 2009. The Sikh celebration of Fateh Divas is held the day after Hindu festival of lights Diwali.[3]

Baba Major Singh

date unknown

Artist Unknown
21st Century

...Baba Major Singh, who's known to have the world's largest dumalla (warrior turban). The turban is made of 1300 feet of fabric. Baba is a Nihang Sikh, an order of monk-warriors[4]

Insp. Baltej Singh Dhillon (Ret.)

20th C

Artist Unknown
21st Century

Insp. Baltej Singh Dhillon is now a 27-year veteran of the RCMP. But when he applied to join the RCMP in 1988, he had to fight for his right to wear a beard and turban.[5]

Endnotes

1. "Muhammad Khan Zaman Khan," Wikipedia Commons (Wikimedia Foundation, July 1, 2022), https://en.wikipedia.org/wiki/Muhammad_Khan_Zaman_Khan.

2. "Sir Arjun Singh, Raja of Narsinghgarh (c. 1900)," Wikipedia Commons (Wikipedia Foundation), accessed November 22, 2022, https://commons.wikimedia.org/wiki/File:Sir_Arjun_Singh,_Raja_of_Narsinghgarh_(c._1900).jpg.

3. "Dastar," The Reader Wiki, Reader View of Wikipedia, 10AD, https://thereaderwiki.com/en/Dastar.

4. "World's Biggest Turban," DangerousMinds, August 4, 2014, https://dangerousminds.net/comments/worlds_biggest_turban.

5. . "The Turban That Rocked the RCMP: How Baltej Singh Dhillon Challenged the RCMP - and Won." CBCnews (CBC/Radio Canada, May 11, 2017), https://www.cbc.ca/2017/canadathestoryofus/the-turban-that-rocked-the-rcmp-how-baltej-singh-dhillon-challenged-the-rcmp-and-won-1.4110271.

Chapter 3

Europe
Slaves in Silk

Having examined the forms of and motivations behind the turban, we are now better equipped to read the "thousand words" encrypted in the proceeding pages.

Considerations

This text begins with the global history of the turban as the American history has been so corrupted or outright hidden. We must therefore ground the foundation of this examination in the oldest information we currently have access to, which ties back to our history in what is today called Europe. This serves the dual purpose of using the colonist's own records to support what the Moors are beginning to salvage from their genetic memory banks.

At the time the following images were painted, Euro-centric government education teaches us the Moors (misnomered negro, black, colored) were at their lowest state and had been for generations, some going so far as to insist our subjugation was divine will. Meanwhile (again contemporary to when these images were rendered) Napoleon I of France was laboring to hide a portion of our legacy of greatness—of which he was well aware beiing beneficiary of the French Caribbean colonies in his possession. While the colonial occupiers distributed media showing our people in rags of checks, calicoes and stripes and other Negro cloths (*See Chapter 4*) their brothers—not cousins—back in Europe were engaging in an

5
Portrait of a black African boy
Flemish or Italian/Venetian School, 18th century
Oil on canvas, not signed

69.5 by 49 cm

Portraits of black Africans were quite popular in the Netherlands during the second half of the 17th and most of the 18th century. Rembrandt, Govert Flinck, Jacques de Gheyn II, Caspar de Crayer, Frans van Mieris, Cornelis Troost and many others made portraits of black Africans. They were often portrayed as young servant boys standing behind a white man or lady, but also as a Moorish prince or king, occasionally. Africans who stayed in Holland as diplomats or students were portrayed but most portraits were studies of anonymous figures. Although the present portrait fits well in the Dutch tradition of portrait paintings of black Africans, because of the Christian cross the boy is holding so prominently it is more likely to be from a catholic country like Flanders or Italy than from calvinist Holland.

6
Artur Kaan (Austrian, 1867 - 1940)
Bronze portrait "Murbruk"
Signed and dated: A. Kaan '95
and Vervielfältigung vorbehalten

Oriental revival (the Oriental School) featuring swarthy Moors decked out in lavish splendor.

If these were supposed to be "stylized" renderings by modern Europeans, why did their imagination depict us in such grandeur? Over the course of time, most of the description included with many of the portraits have been abridged with many of them being tainted with the prejudices of the authors. One example is that of Giacomo Casanova (*page 22*) where, despite being painted by and mentioned in the journal of a prince, the subject is today reported as a random African the prince elected to dress in tailored silks, then spend months, if not years, painting.[1] This omission of such details offers the Moors an opportunity to fill in their own blanks.

Moors depicted in acts of hospitality has been corrupted to imply they were enslaved. The slave theory is usually based on the observer's association of dark skin with servitude, where a reasonable person would focus more on the attire than the attired and see, **clearly**: this is not a slave. Unfortunately, hate is blinding. Add to this the number of these "slaves" rendered in paintings which again, took no less than months to complete wearing silks, linens, exotic feathers, jewels, and precious metals—it becomes evident that these were not captives. The portrait of Christiaan vanMolhoop exemplifies how Eurocentric sources would have one believe that servants were dressed in regalia such as feathers and ruffles.[2] This man vanMalhoop, dressed in such finery, displaying such arrogance, is reportedly a coach-man, dressed as he is

to demonstrate the eccentricity and wealth of the his Dutch master. Referring again to research, his attitude has been accredited to the protection afforded by his master's social status. Unfortunately, the red-white-and-blue of his turban's costly plumage indicates there is much more going on than purported — or admitted — by curators. When vanMalhop's portrait was painted, red, white and blue were the colors of the Grand Duchy of Luxembourg, a Dutch protectorate.[3] It would have to be an eccentric nobleman indeed to dress in a manner indistinguishable from his coachman–and have said coachman's portrait painted. It should be noted that circa 1909, this work was cataloged under another title: *The African Prince*.[4] Additionally and again, why is this "servant" wearing the turban; a recognized symbol of nobility, scholarship, and divinity?

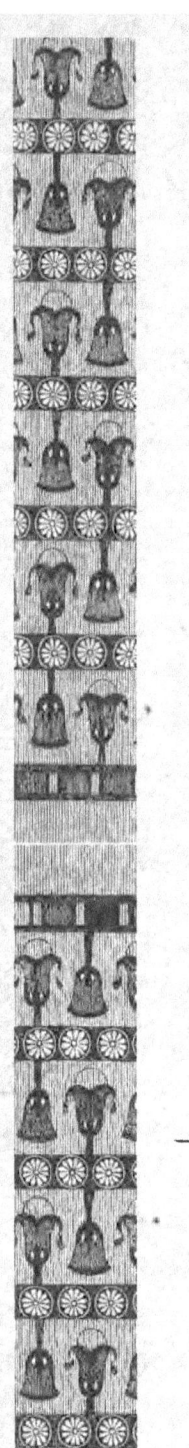

There is nothing wrapped in my turban but God,
– Mansur Al-Hallaj

Moorish Merchant
Campo dei Mori
(Moors Square)
13th Century

Artist Unknown

Portrait of a Man

(Self-portrait?)
1433

Jan van Eyck
Belgian, 1390–1441

The sitter's clothing is that of a prosperous individual. Most striking is his flamboyant red hat – a chaperon, a headdress for men fashionable in the fifteenth century. The hood, which usually hung down over the wearer's neck and shoulders, has been piled up on top of the sitter's head, the long tail wound around it.[5]

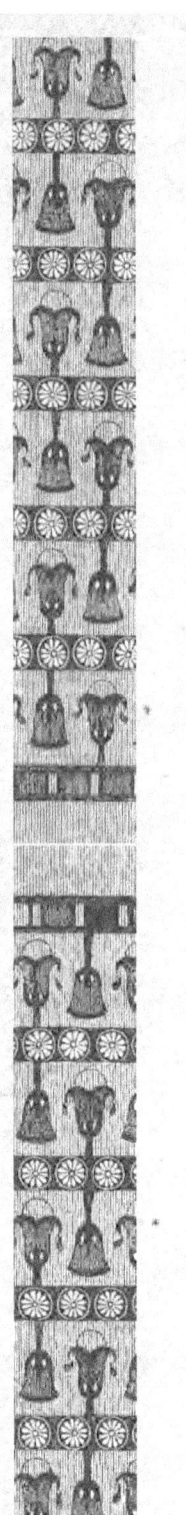

Shams was the wind that would blow the scholar's turban off from Rumi's head, and turn a quiet academic into an enthusiastic lover of God.
— ACihan Okuyucu

"The Adoration of the Magi"

Detail showing the magus Balthazar
1480 - 1490

Georges Trubert
French, 15th Century

I'm a Sikh; it's part of my religious tradition to never cut my hair and keep it wrapped in a turban.
– Waris Ahluwalia

Adoration of the Magi

Detail showing the magus Balthazar
1495–1505

Andrea Mantegna
Italian, c. 1431 - 1506

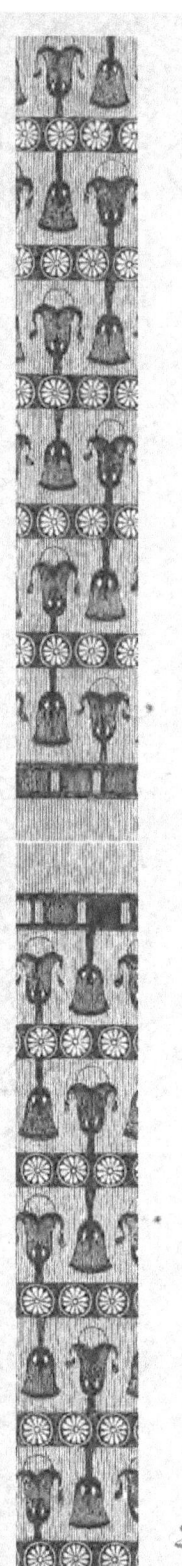

He was wearing Professor Quirrell's turban, which kept talking to him, telling him he must transfer to Slytherin at once, because it was his destiny.
— J.K. Rowling

Moor in a Turban
1629

Jan Lievens
Dutch, 1607 - 1674

I eat too much. I drink to much. A greedy selfish such-n-such. But when I wrap my turban on my mind is clear, I'm 'Baba Lon'.
— Lon Milo DuQuette

Man in Oriental Costume

c. 1635

Rembrandt van Rijn
Dutch, 1606 - 1669

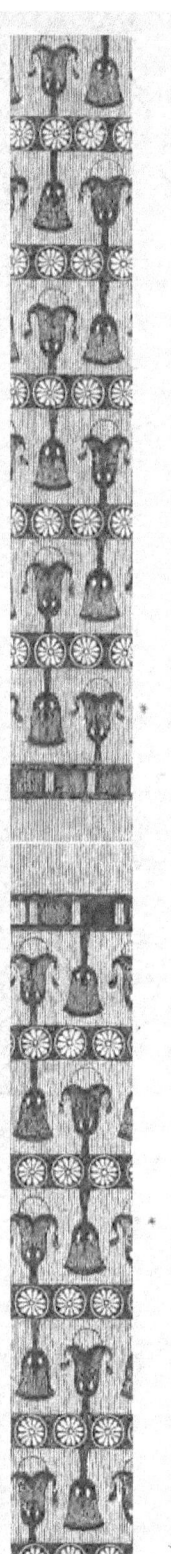

Adoration of the Magi (Stockolm)

Detail showing the magus Balthazar 1633-1639

Matthias Stom Dutch, c. 1600 - 1652(?)

"Caspar"
1640 - 1650

Jan Van Bijlert
Dutch, 1597–1671

Adorned with stunning jewels and lustrous pearls, Caspar wears a turban centered by a cameo of a man in prayer, likely in reference to the overall narrative of the scene – the adoration of the Magi. In his hands, he holds a silver beaker of frankincense that is reminiscent of the work of the famed silversmith Adam van Vianen, who was active in Utrecht during the same period. Crafted in irregular, organic forms that presaged the Art Nouveau style, goblets and beakers by van Vianen were highly sought after by leading Dutch families. Van Bijlert's inclusion of the form here not only indicates the wealth of his subject, King Caspar but also reveals the artist's mindfulness of the tastes of his wealthy clientele. His nod to contemporary fashions and prevailing tastes ensured his continuous popularity throughout his lifetime.[6]

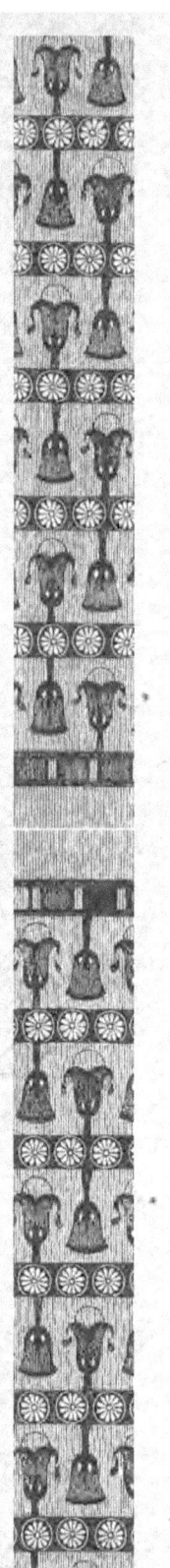

Moor Wearing a Turban and Armour

c. 1640 - 1670

Karel van Mander III
Dutch, 1609–1670

...wearing a turban of yellow, signifying knowledge, and a robe of purple, portraying purity and activity, Virchand Gandhi of Bombay delivered a lecture on the religions of India..... - Author: The New York Times

Moorish Nobleman

15th Century

Artist Unknown

Turbans are exchanged as a sign of respect or friendship as well.
– Mahaveer Singh, a tour guide from Jodhpur, 2015

An African Woman

c. 1710–1715

Willem van Mieris
Dutch, 1662–1747

"Set against a green background, an African woman wears a coral-colored turban, a prominent feather affixed with a gem clip. The textures are finely rendered, the gem and pearls shine, while her face and arm are particularly well modeled, marble-like.."[7]

I would rather see a Turkish turban in the midst of the City [i.e., Constantinople] than the Latin mitre
— Author: Loukas Notaras

[One of]
The Mentmore Busts

c. 1715

N. P. Severin
Venetian, 18th Century

These magnificent black-a-moor busts in the choicest marbles with beautiful gilt-bronze embellishments and well executed carving reflect the taste for busts of blackamoors in varied clothing and headdress carved from multicoloured marbles, alabasters and porphyry which became increasingly popular during the seventeenth century...These busts constituted important decorative elements of the residences of 18th and early 19th century connoisseurs, demonstrating not only their owner's taste but also their cultured and extensive travels.[8]

Adoration of the King

Detail showing the magus Balthazar

Early 16th Century

Jan Gossaert
Dutch, 1478-1532

An archer in a turbanned headdress

The head of a Moor [former title]

c. 1730-40

Giovanni Battista Piazzetta
Austrian, 1682-1754

A black and white chalk drawing of a young man, holding a bow and wearing a silk turban and jewelled earring.

It is not possible to know the identity of the sitter in this drawing, but it possibly shows a model of North African descent, who has evidently been dressed in 'exotic' costume in the artist's studio.⁹

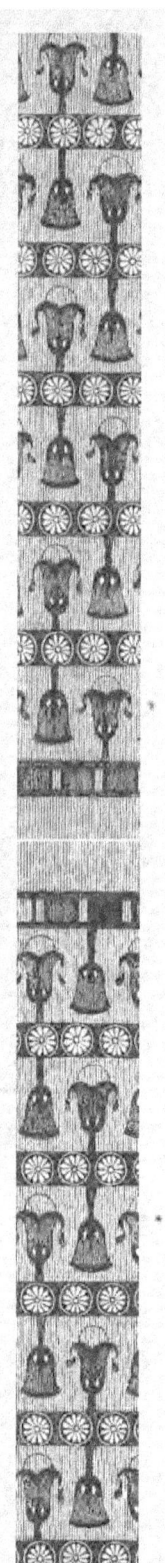

Jean-Etienne Liotard
Self Portrait

Portrait of a Young Woman [Rachael Baptiste]

c. late 18thC

Jean-Etienne Liotard
Swiss, 1702 - 1789

Study of a [Black]* Boy

c. 1827–38

William Etty
English, 1787 - 1849

Search of United States-based sources yielded "Study of a Black Boy." Portrait is recorded in England/ artist's homeland as "Study of a Boy."

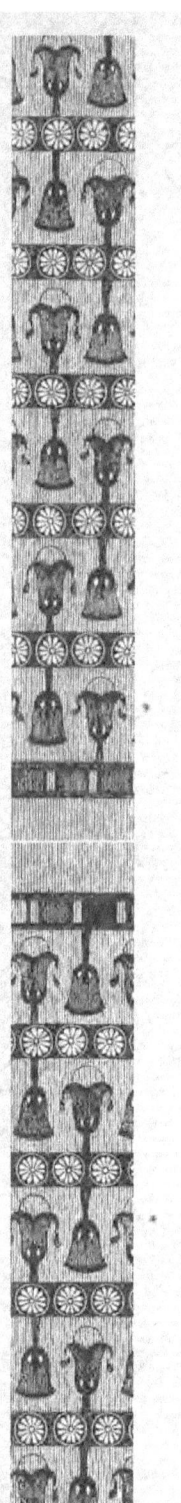

I am still not used to being the possessor of such a grand title. I believe I shall have to start wearing a purple satin turban and carrying a lorgnette.
– Mary Balogh

Christiaan van Molhoop
Circa 1795

Ozias Humphry
British, 1742–1810

As usual, the oldest women were the most decorated, and the ugliest the most conspicuous. If there was a beautiful lily, or a sweet rose, you had to search for it, concealed in some corner behind a mother with a turban, or an aunt with a bird of paradise.
– Alexandre Dumas

Giacomo Casanova
aka
Portrait of a Young Black Italian Man
Circa 1795

Prince Charles de Ligne
Belgian, 1735–1814

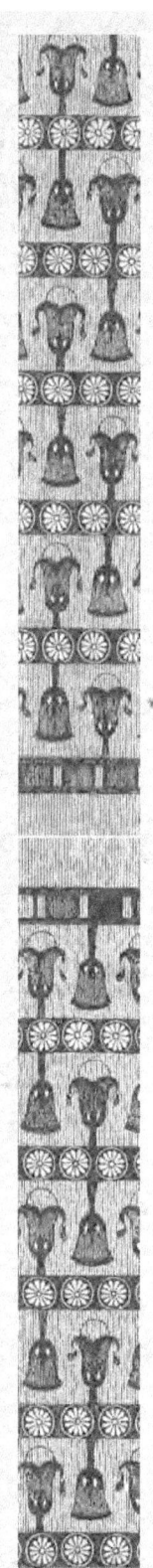

The Orange Seller

c. 1827–38

Ludwig Deutsch
English, 1787 - 1849

Le Jeune Ottoman

date unknown

Hans Johan Fredrik Berg
Norwegian, 1813–1874

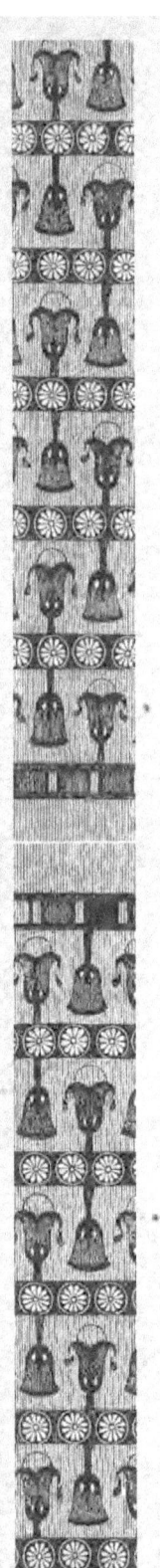

Portrait of a Moorish servant in classical hunting dress and a turban

19thC

Circle of
Jonathan Richardson
British, ca. 1665–1745

...shown wearing a turban and elegant silk clothes next to a falcon cage.[10]

Orientalist Oil On Canvas Moorish Princess

19thC

Unsigned
[After Alessandro Tiarini
Italian, 1577–1668]

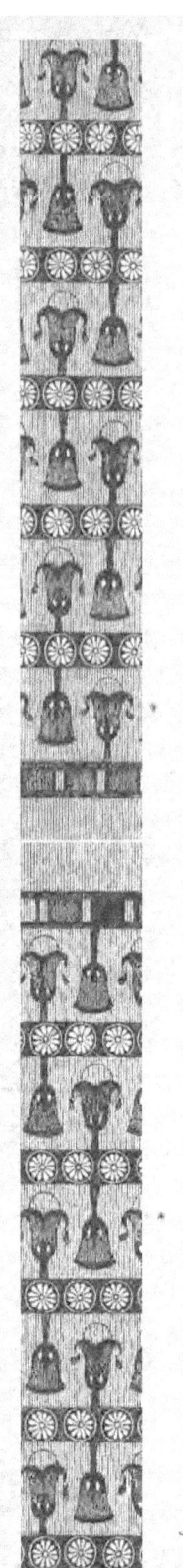

The Fruit Bearer
1844

William Derby
British, 1786 - 1847

The Guard

date unknown

Georges Cairn
French, 1843-1919

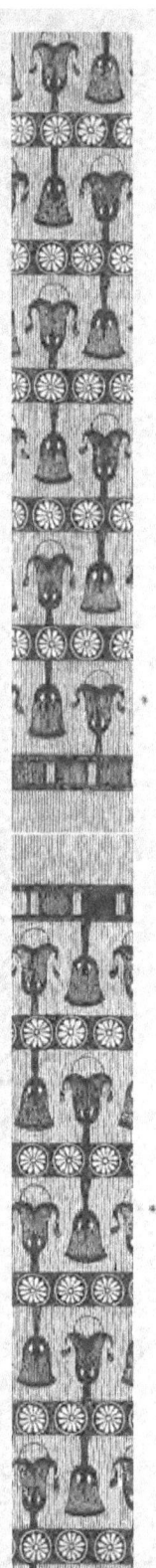

Bashi-Bazouk

c. 1868–69

Jan Van Bijlert
Dutch, 1597–1671

Sources claim that the artist collected various artifacts in his travels throughout the East. Upon his return home, he hired models to wear curated costumes reflecting what he imagined to be the past—again, according to sources. Even if that were so, and these were models, why use Moors, and not the pale-skinned Arabs depicted in many modern texts?[11]

Moorish Chief

1879

John Everett Millais
English, 1829–1896

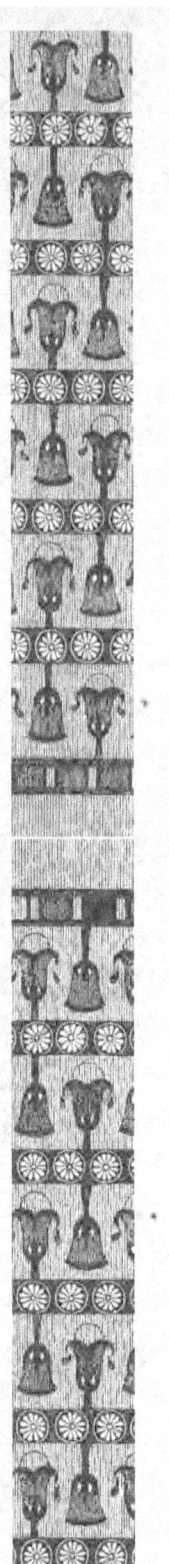

The Inspection

1883

Ludwig Deutsch
Austrian, 1855-1935

Here Deutsch shows an Arab man in a striped kaftan and turban examining a late Indian or Qajar Iranian helmet, with two Ottoman-style pistols in his belt. Another pistol and a sword with a flared ivory grip called a yataghan lie on the inlaid mother-of-pearl table. A bow harp is subtly visible beside the figure's embroidered shoe, an interesting addition to a scene otherwise filled with weapons. An ostrich egg also lies on the floor, next to a manuscript in an Ottoman gilt-stamped leather binding.[12]

In this market every head has a different fancy: everyone winds his turban in a different fashion.
– Saib Tabrizi

The Connoisseurs

Circa 1900

Jean Discart Italian, 1855-1940

Type Marocain

1905

Marie José Jean Raymond Silbert
French, 1862-1935

The Treasure Chest

1920

Jan Van Bijlert
Dutch, 1597–1671

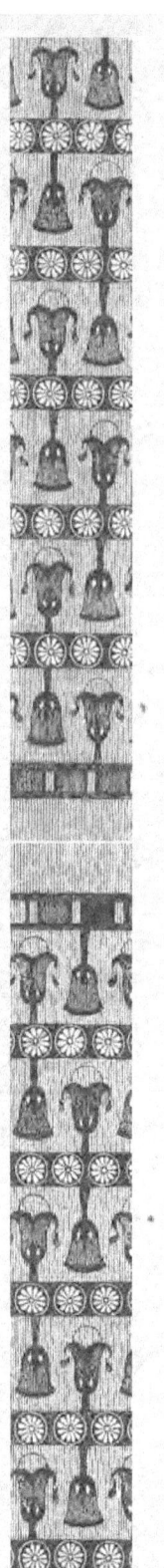

The Goza Smoker

1884

Ludwig Deutsch
Austrian, 1855-1935

> In the present work, Deutsch turns his ethnographic eye to a familiar and enduring motif in Orientalist art, the Arab smoker in idle repose...
>
> The man in Deutsch's painting wears a traditional striped qumbaz beneath a heavier outer robe...
> The formidable doorway behind the Arab figure – likely the entrance to a private palace rather than a mosque or madrasa, given the man's apparently inebriated state - offers evidence of Deutsch's extensive use of well-known pattern books and popular prints.[13]

Vintage Mid-Century Ceramic Lady Head Vase, Planter, with Turban and Gold Hoop Earrings, Gold Accents

c. 1950

Lefton Exclusives
Japan, 20th Century

Moor Woman Head with Stripped Blue and Green Turban

c 2020

Alessi Ceramiche
Italian, 1955-Present

> Part of the Heritage collection, this handcrafted vase by Giacomo Alessi expresses the lyrical beauty of Sicily's artistic and cultural traditions. The Moor woman's comely visage is characterized by a bright color palette and sculptural details: rich black complexion, a striped blue-and-green turban, relief detailing in the bold eyebrows and locks of black hair, and orange accents for the expressive eyes, lips, and earrings.

Keeping 'pure focused applied awareness of the Self (Soul)' (shuddha upayog) is the same as being in the Absolute Supreme Self-form (Parmatma swaroop).
– Dada Bhagwan

Moor's Head with Light Blue Turban

21st Century

D.D. Ceramiche
Siciliane
Italy, 21st Century

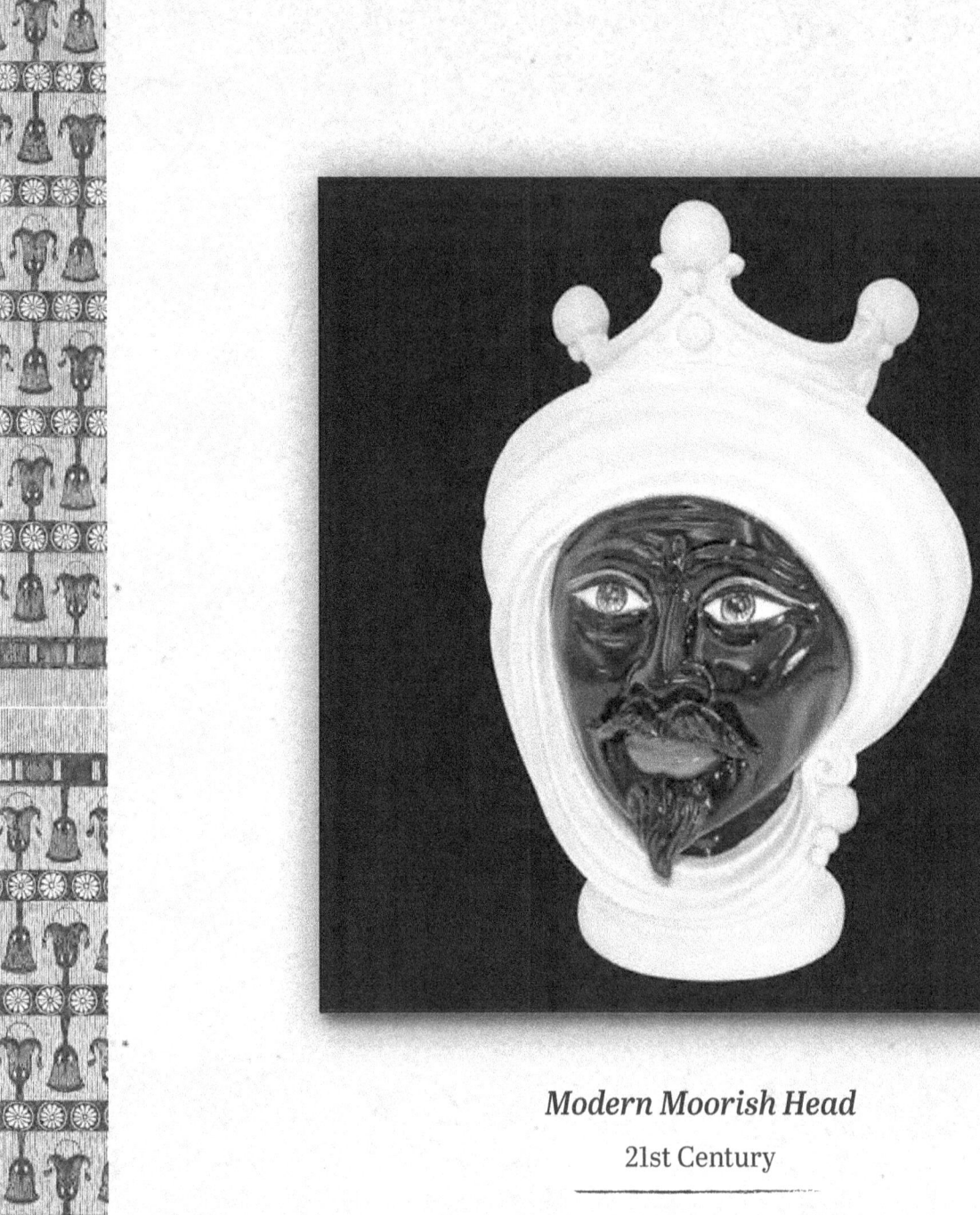

Modern Moorish Head

21st Century

Sofia Ceramiche di Caltagirone
21st Century

Heads of Moor Luis

21st Century

D.D. Ceramiche Siciliane
Italy, 21st Century

Moorish Head De Bellis Dec. Turquoise

21st Century

Pascal Ceramiche d'Arte Ravello
Italy, 21st Century

Heads of Moor [Afro]

21st Century

D.D. Ceramiche Siciliane
Italy, 21st Century

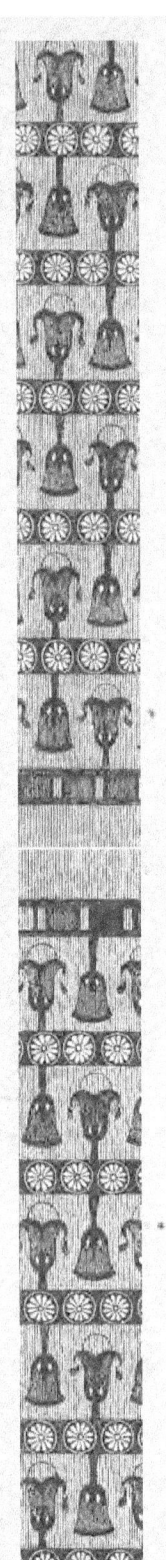

Pair of Moors Heads
21st Century

Ceramiche di Caltagirone Gioielli Bomboniere
Sicilian, 21st Century

18kt Gold Gem-set Blackamoor Brooch

20th Century

Giulio Nardi
Italian, 1897 – 1976

18kt Gold Gem-set Blackamoor Brooch, Nardi, wearing an elaborate vest with full-cut diamonds and channel-set sapphires, and sapphire and diamond turban, lg. 1 1/2 in., signed G. Nardi.

Estimate $2,000-3,000[15]

This amazing original set of Antique Blackamoor 18K Yellow Gold Brooch & Earrings are circa 1890. They are the best of the best! The faces on the Brooch and Earrings are made out of Chalcedony or Onyx. This is instead of enamel over metal, or wood that deteriorates. They are very difficult to carve and this is why Blackamoors such as Nardi and others went to wood or enamel over metal.

These earrings were carved by a master carver over 100 years ago. To find a matching set of any Blackamoors is rare, but to find original Onyx

Antique Blackamoor 18K Yellow Gold Brooch and Earrings covered in Sapphires
c. 1890

Artist Unknown
19th Century

carved set is even rarer. As a matter of fact, I have never seen another set like this. The Diamonds are old European cut VS clarity and G for color and the Sapphires are a deep blue. Carved and detailed in 18K Yellow Gold body with a double clip back for the brooch and European pierced back for the earrings.

This comes with a Certificate of Appraisal for $22,166.00.[16]

The Regency era — a fashion said to be inspired by the increased trade with India, took hold of the turban style, making a statement of class and wealth. In these days the style of turban was initially simple, but as its popularity grew and hair styles became more elaborate so did the styles of turban. The headpieces would often be decorated with jewels and worn to evening balls and functions. - Lindsay Judge

Coral and diamond blackamoor brooch

20th Century

Giulio Nardi
Italian, 1897 – 1976

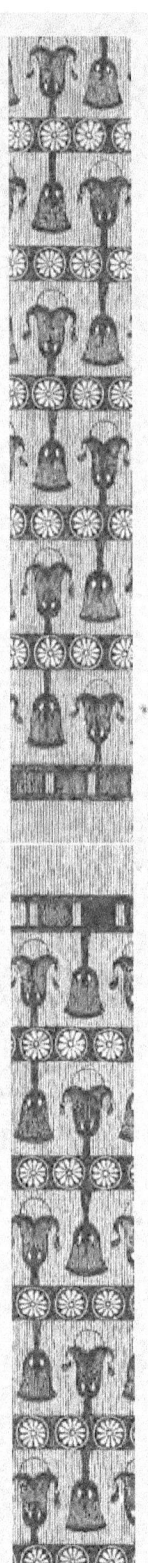

i.i.mcdxcii This painting can be found on the Metropolitan Museum of Art's website at www.metmuseum.org.

TITLE: "The Abduction of Rebecca by a Knight Templar"

"The subject is drawn from Sir Walter Scott's Ivanhoe (1820), in which the knight Templar Brian de Bois-Guilbert, together with his Saracen slave and the Jewish heroine Rebecca, escape from the burning Torquilstone Castle. This painting is a reduced variant of one completed in 1828 and exhibited at the Salon of 1831 (Wallace Collection, London). The eclectic mix of exotic types, medieval themes, and dramatic action was a mainstay of Romanticism; a later rendition of this subject by Cogniet's contemporary Eugene Delacroix is also in the Metropolitan's collection (03.30)."

I must add that it is not actually known whether or not the Saracen (Moor) who's riding one of the signs of what Christians called "Moorishness", the "pure white" horse presumably a "White Arabian Horse", is actually a "slave" or not.

It's important to know that if a Moor was to become a slave to a Christian that he'd be classified as a "Moosco" or "little Moor", and a "Converso" (convert) and he'd not be allowed to wear silks of any kind, and sometimes we were even prohibited from wearing sandals, turbans, or jewelry.

Seeing how the man above is wearing everything a slave is not supposed to wear under Christian captivity, I'd say the detailing of the scene has a strong element of current racial bias. Continuing the idea that "blacks" have never been anything but slaves.

In fact even though the painting is attributed to the Frenchman Léon Cogniet, it is actually not known when or who painted the image and for what reason.

All that has been agreed upon concerning this painting is pure speculation. The point being whenever you read descriptions of "blacks", "Moors", "Hamites", etc. be sure to analyze the image yourself.

Anything concerning the Moors will be accompanied with tons of fallacies and erroneous consensuses.

#Maur #Maure #Mouro #Moor #Saracen #Saraceni #NIPMEDIA

Endnotes

1. Röell Guus, "5. Portrait of a Black African Boy," in *Uit Verre Streken: Luxury Goods from Dutch Trading Posts in the West Indies, East Indies, China, Japan and Africa, 17th-19th Centuries* (Maastricht: Guus Röell, 2018), 10-11.

2. Ozias Humphry, *Christiaan Van Molhoop*, 1795, Tate Museum, London.

3. "Flag of Luxembourg," Encyclopædia Britannica (Encyclopædia Britannica, inc.), accessed October 19, 2022, https://www.britannica.com/topic/flag-of-Luxembourg.

4. Tate, "'Christiaan Van Molhoop', Ozias Humphry, C.1795," Tate (Tate Museum, December 31, 1794), https://www.tate.org.uk/art/artworks/humphry-christiaan-van-molhoop-t13796.

5. The National Gallery, "Jan Van Eyck, Portrait of a Man (Self Portrait?)," Jan van Eyck | Portrait of a Man (Self Portrait?) | NG222 (National Gallery, London, January 1, 1970), https://www.nationalgallery.org.uk/paintings/jan-van-eyck-portrait-of-a-man-self-portrait.

6. "Jan Van Bijlert: Caspar (1640-1650)," Artsy, accessed August 22, 2022, https://www.artsy.net/artwork/jan-van-bijlert-caspar.

7. "Noma Displays an African Tronie from the Dutch Golden Age," New Orleans Museum of Art, April 22, 2020, https://noma.org/noma-acquires-an-african-tronie-from-the-dutch-golden-age/.

8. "A Pair of Tortoiseshell Inlaid Premtalian Gilt-Bronze-Mounted Marble Busts of Blackamoors… Stamped N. P. Severin, Régence, circa 1715," Sothebys.com, accessed November 23, 2022, https://www.sothebys.com/en/auctions/ecatalogue/2010/treasures-aristocratic-heirlooms-l10307/lot.6.html.

9. "Giovanni Battista Piazzetta (1682-1754) - An Archer in a Turbanned Headdress," Royal Collection Trust, accessed October 23, 2022, https://www.rct.uk/collection/990755/an-archer-in-a-turbanned-headdress.

10. "Orientalist Oil on Canvas Moorish Princess," LiveAuctioneers, accessed September 23, 2022, https://www.liveauctioneers.com/item/79597244_orientalist-oil-on-canvas-moorish-princess.

11. "Bashi-Bazouk Ca. 1868–69 Jean-Léon Gérôme French," Metmuseum.org, accessed October 23, 2022, https://www.metmuseum.org/art/collection/search/651837.

12. "Ludwig Deutsch - The Inspection 1883," Sothebys.com, accessed October 23, 2022, https://www.sothebys.com/en/auctions/ecatalogue/2010/19th-century-european-art-n08673/lot.7.html.

13. Emily M Weeks, "Ludwig Deutsch (Austrian, 1855-1935) the Goza Smoker," Bonhams, accessed October 24, 2022, https://www.bonhams.com/auction/25444/lot/65/ludwig-deutsch-austrian-1855-1935-the-goza-smoker/.

14. "Muhammad Khan Zaman Khan," Wikipedia Commons (Wikimedia Foundation, July 1, 2022), https://en.wikipedia.org/wiki/Muhammad_Khan_Zaman_Khan.

15. "Sold at Auction 18kt Gold Gem-Set Blackamoor Brooch, Nardi Auction Number 2693b Lot Number 394: Skinner Auctioneers," Skinner Inc., accessed October 24, 2022, https://www.skinnerinc.com/auctions/2693B/lots/394.

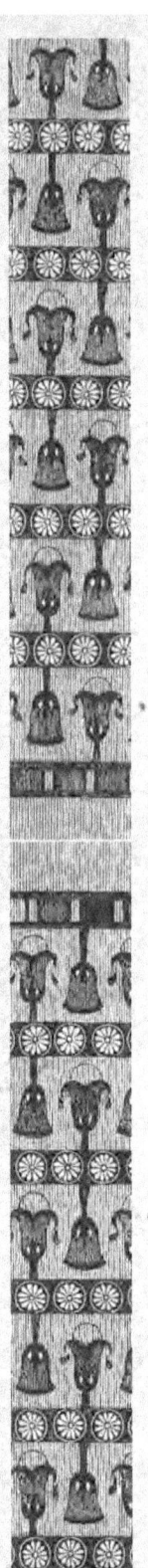

16. "Antique Blackamoor 18k Yellow Gold Brooch and Earrings," Cris Notti Jewels, September 18, 2019, https://www.crisnottijewels.com/product/antique-blackamoor-18k-yellow-gold-brooch-earrings/.

17. *TITLE:* "*The Abduction of Rebecca by a Knight Templar,*" photograph, *Instagram.com* (@i.i.mcdxcii, March 5, 2022), https://www.instagram.com/i.i.mcdxcii/.

Chapter 4

Africa America
Land of the FreeMan

Negro Cloth

"If we would agree to take the Fezzes and Turbans off the Moors' heads and remove the sandals from their feet and enforce severe punishments, and to also swear a death o...ath between ourselves to religiously and faithfully not to allow anyone to teach the Moorish children who they really were or who their forefathers were, and only allow the Moorish children to be taught that they were truly Negroes, Black people, and Colored folks, 200 years from today the Moorish people would not know their nationality nor the national name of their forefathers. Also they would not know from which land or ancestors that they are descended from."

Prior to the Fall of the Moors in Granada, the turban was a common–and unifying–sight across the Moorish Empire which spanned Northwest and Southwest Amexum and it's adjoining islands. Once guided to the "New World" by Moorish prisoners, the conspiracy to cut the Moors of America off from being a nation was an enterprise engaged in at all levels by the European colonists. Examination of the time and effort expended to ensure the oppression of the indigenous Moors while turning a profit was nothing less than astounding. The Three-Fifths Compromise was codified in the Constitution for the United States to the deny the Moors access to their religion and nationality, leaving their mind, body, and spirit to be enslaved by the occupying nations of Europe until 1865.[1,2] This Compromise was preceded by the South Carolina Negro Act in 1735, wherein colonial Englishmen enacted legislation outlining which textiles would be used to clothe the captive Moors.[3] These textiles would be imported from England as well as other English colonies using cotton grown and harvested by the enslaved Moors on their own land.[4] Part of this subjugation included the removal of their fez and turban in an attempt to further separate them from their birthright. Fortunately, having practiced some habits for so long as to render them instinct, the Moors—especially the women—continued to wrap their hair in the fashion of their ancestors despite the concerted effort to make them forget. How unfortunate they were forced to do so using inferior cloth sourced from their enslavement and birthright theft.

To take away the turban meant subjugating a person and humiliating him[7]

Tignon Laws

Ironically, while English colonists–turned–occupiers were suppressing Moorish turbans, French and Spanish colonists were imposing them. In an effort to appease the insecurities of so-called white women, Tignon Laws were enacted to compel so-called Negro and mulatto women to wrap their "exotic" hair. In true Moorish fashion, the women under this mandate converted attempted humiliation into haute couture. Since the tignon laws forced the covering of the hair and forbade the wearing of jewels or any other indication of status or wealth, they took to wrapping their hair in elaborate manners using various knots.[5] Ironically—again—this his had the opposite effect intended by the tignon laws as it made these women of color even more exotic and even more attractive to the men these head-rags were meant to repel.[6]

Portraits of vaious women sujected to Tignon Laws in the 18th Century[8]

Turbans after Reconstruction

Between the Civil War and the Jim Crow Era of the United States was the period known as Reconstruction when, via the 13th and 14th Amendments as well as the Dawes Rolls, the Moors were further delayed in reclaiming their birthright. Reconstruction gave way to the Jim Crow apartheid era where using the wrong accommodations or speaking to the wrong person could land a Moor in a grave. One means to get around this hazard was to wrap a turban if one ran the risk of engaging with colonial savages. Sleepy-headed Moors thinking they were donning disguises by wearing turban were actually invoking the powers of their forebearers; while they may not have known its significance, those they were seeking to deceive certainly did: during this era, it was common in media to recognize a soothsayer, fortune teller, or wise man by his turban.

The following images are examples of turbans worn across the Maghreb before, during, and after the colonial occupation of Moorish America.

John Redd, aka Korla Pandit, first so-called negro with a television show who passed as Hindoo.[9]

Tuareg Man in Blue

date unknown

Artist Unknown
21st Century

The most striking attribute of the tradition dress of the Tuareg is the indigo veil, worn by the men but not the women, giving rise to the popular name the Blue Men of the Sahara, or Men of the Veil. Men begin wearing a veil at the age 25. The portion of the turban covering the face, or litham, functions as a shield against the harsh desert elements, but can be found in the military costumes of Al Andalus.[10]

Turbans are a source of mystery — and, all too often, terrible misunderstanding — to those who don't wear them.
-Rupindar Singh

The Illustrious & Magnificent Sharif Mulay Al Rashid

c. 1694

Nicolas de Larmessin
1632-1694

Free Women of Color with their Children and Servants in a Landscape

c 1770-1796

Agostino Brunias
Italian 1730-1796

Dido Elizabeth Belle Lindsay
c. 1778

David Martin
Scottish 1737 -1797

7. It is said in Cherokee country that Sequoyah didn't really pose for King's portrait. Regardless of whether this is true, the clothing that the subject of the painting is wearing is consistent with the kinds of clothing Sequoyah reportedly wore. Bryan Giemza argues that in King's portrait Sequoyah is "wearing a tignon more commonly associated with blacks and the Caribbean fringe, but perhaps a more generic signifier of racial otherness" (143). Giemza misunderstands the context. As Perdue argues, "Most southern Indians, whether 'mixed blood' or 'full blood,' expressed their identity through the clothes they wore, which were a mixture of Native and European styles but exhibited remarkable unity across the South"; turbans were among the accepted "Indian" clothes for southern tribes at the time the portrait was first produced ("Race" 714). In reality, rather than signifying Sequoyah's "racial otherness," his turban confirms his Indianness.

Sequoyah

c. 1836

C.B. King
United States-ian
1785 - 1862

Originally the head-wrap, or turban, was worn by both enslaved men and women. In time, however, it became almost exclusively a female accessory. In the photograph above, the women wear head-wraps, while the men wear hats.[12]

Mammy represented wholesomeness. You can trust the mammy pitchwoman.[14]

Evidence from the 1915 Court Case: Aunt Jemima Mills Company v. Rigney and Company[13]

Jim Crow Museum Ferris State University

Pair of Vintage Aunt Jemima and Uncle Mose Salt & Pepper Shakers[15]

John Roland Redd aka Korla Pandit
1921-1998

Fantasy Records
United States 1958

In the United States in the 1920s there were two classes of people who could pull off a turban: "Oriental" men and fashionable "white women". This fact points to a curious relationship between these two groups, especially in the context of the alternative spiritual scene of the time. South Asian men presenting themselves as yogis were gendered in consistently contradictory ways. They were both feminine in their appearance and sensibilities and hyper-masculine when it came to their sexuality. In the popular imagination they were painted as wily con-artists. Their usual victims were the wealthy white women who constituted the majority of their audiences. However, as yoga began to blend into the domestic metaphysical schools of Theosophy and New Thought, American women quickly co-opted not only the aesthetics but also the imagined authority of their South Asian teachers, becoming "Mahatmas" in their own right.[16]

The Hebrew word mitznefet has been translated as "mitre" (KJV) or "headdress". It was most likely a "turban", as the word comes from the root "to wrap."[7]

Rabbi Arnold Josiah Ford
1877-1935

Artist Unknown

Endnotes

1. U.S. Constitution, art. 1, sec. 2, cl. 3.

2. U.S. Constitution, amend. 14, sec. 1.

3. "NPS Ethnography: African American Heritage & Ethnography," National Parks Service (U.S. Department of the Interior), accessed October 18, 2022, https://www.nps.gov/ethnography/aah/aaheritage/lowCountryc.htm.

4. *Who Got Paid to Help Keep Slaves? Colonial Indictments & Another #MessedUpMoorishStory* (Califa Media Publishing, 2022), https://youtu.be/KPsgnzYTeYA.

5. Samantha Callender, "The Tignon Laws Set the Precedent for the Appropriation and Misconception around Black Hair," Essence (Essence, October 24, 2020), https://www.essence.com/hair/tignon-laws-cultural-appropriation-black-natural-hair/.

6. Karen Harris, "Tignon Laws Forced Black Women to Cover Their Hair," History Daily, July 25, 2020, https://historydaily.org/tignon-laws-facts-trivia-stories.

7. Neutral Singh, "Heritage of the Turban," Sikh Philosophy Network (Sikh Philosophy Network, August 2, 2004), https://www.sikhphilosophy.net/threads/heritage-of-the-turban.440/.

8. Jarnell Dorman, "Tignon Law: The Attempted Oppression of African Beauty," ecoterie beauty (ecoterie beauty, September 26, 2020), https://www.ecoteriebeauty.co/blog/tignonlaw.

9. Kudjo Adwo El, "National Headdress," in Hold Me Up: Noble Drew Ali's Lessons on Law & Spirituality, ed. Tauheedah Najee-Ullah El (Lafayette, IN: Califa Media Publishing, 2021), pp. 60-64

10. David Nicolle and Angus McBride, in *The Moors: The Islamic West 7th-15th Century AD* (Oxford: Osprey Military, 2008), 45, 47.

11. Rose Gubele, "Utalotsa Woni—'Talking Leaves': A Re-Examination of the Cherokee Syllabary and Sequoyah," *Studies in American Indian Literatures* 24, no. 4 (2012): p. 47, https://doi.org/10.5250/studamerindilite.24.4.0047.

12. "Slavery and the Making of America . the Slave Experience: Men, Women & Gender: PBS," Slavery and the Making of America . The Slave Experience: Men, Women & Gender | PBS, accessed October 26, 2022, https://www.thirteen.org/wnet/slavery/experience/gender/feature6.html.

13. H. Parkins, "Aunt Jemima, What Took You so Long?," National Archives and Records Administration (National Archives and Records Administration), accessed October 18, 2022, https://prologue.blogs.archives.gov/2011/08/03/aunt-jemima-what-took-you-so-long/.

14. David Pilgram, "The Mammy Caricature," Ferris State University, October 2000, https://www.ferris.edu/HTMLS/news/jimcrow/mammies/homepage.htm.

15. "Aunt Jemima and Uncle Mose Salt and Pepper Shakers - Nov 21, 2009: Mosby & Co.. Auctions in MD," LiveAuctioneers, accessed November 26, 2022, https://www.liveauctioneers.com/item/6820686_338-aunt-jemima-and-uncle-mose-salt-and-pepper-shakers.

16. Anya Pokazanyeva Foxen, "Turbans, Certain to Charm! South Asian Men, White Women, and the Gendering of Early American Yoga," Interdisciplinary Humanities Center UCSB, May 22, 2017, https://ihc.ucsb.edu/turbans-certain-to-charm/.

17. "Priestly Turban," Wikipedia (Wikimedia Foundation, May 12, 2022), https://en.wikipedia.org/wiki/Priestly_turban.

CHAPTER 5

Prophet Noble Drew Ali's Holy Crown

Gratitude to the Moors for their input on the metaphysics behind the turban worn by the Prophet Noble Drew Ali during the first National Convention of the Moorish Science Temple of America. Adding to the information already presented, we now look at the Prophet's Holy Crown better able to decipher some of the significance behind it. Included are the notes of learned Moors--a fitting sign and proof of the national unity encouraged by our Prophet.

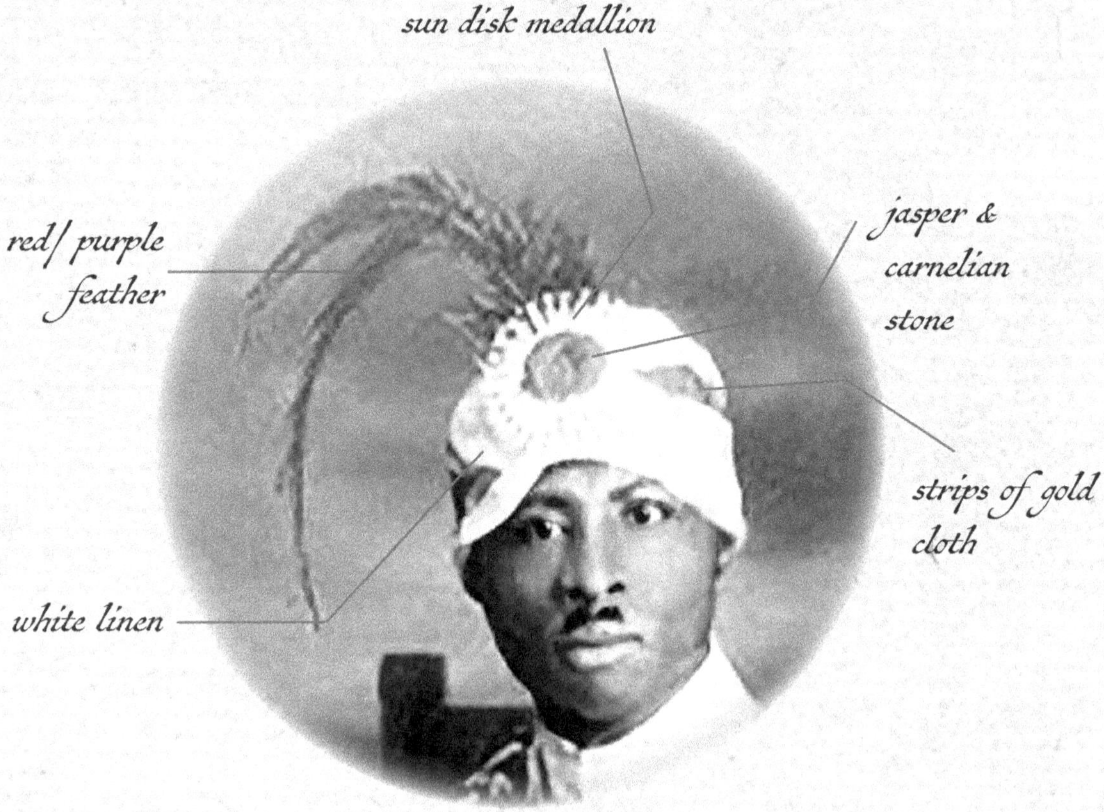

sun disk medallion

red/purple feather

jasper & carnelian stone

strips of gold cloth

white linen

Revelations 4:3

Holman Bible

and the One seated looked like jasper and carnelian stone. A rainbow that looked like an emerald surrounded the throne.

from the notes of
Bro. Kasir Effie Raj El

³ To receive the instruction of wisdom, justice, and judgment, and equity;

⁴ To give subtilty to the simple, to the young man knowledge and discretion.

⁵ A wise *man* will hear, and will increase learning; and a man of understanding shall attain unto wise counsels:

⁶ To understand a proverb, and the interpretation; the words of the wise, and their dark sayings.

⁷ The fear of the LORD *is* the beginning of knowledge: *but* fools despise wisdom and instruction.

The Enticement of Sin

⁸ My son, hear the instruction of thy father, and forsake not the law of thy mother:

⁹ For they *shall be* an ornament of grace unto thy head, and chains about thy neck.

¹⁰ My son, if sinners entice thee, consent thou not.

¹¹ If they say, Come with us, let us lay wait for blood, let us lurk privily for the innocent without cause:

◀ 🔍 Leviticus 8:9 ALL ▶

New American Standard Bible
He also placed the turban on his head, and on the turban, at its front, he placed the golden plate, the holy crown, just as the LORD had commanded Moses.

King James Version
And he put the mitre upon his head; also upon the mitre, *even* upon his forefront, did he put the golden plate, the holy crown; as the LORD commanded Moses.

Holman Bible
He also put the turban on his head and placed the gold medallion, the holy diadem, on the front of the turban, as the LORD had commanded Moses.

International Standard Version
then he set the turban on his head. On the turban at the front he set the golden plate, the sacred crown that the LORD had commanded.

Hard to find Translations that word it correc

Parallel Verses

Holman Bible
Fasten it to a cord of blue yarn so it can be placed on the turban; the medallion is to be on the front of the turban.

New American Standard Bible
You shall fasten it on a blue cord, and it shall be on the turban; it shall be at the front of the turban.

Proverbs 1:5-9 It references the turban Pendent as blissing earned from Following the Fathers Instructions and honoring the Mothers Law... "Thy Deys will be long on the Earthplane as well" symbology of the Pendent

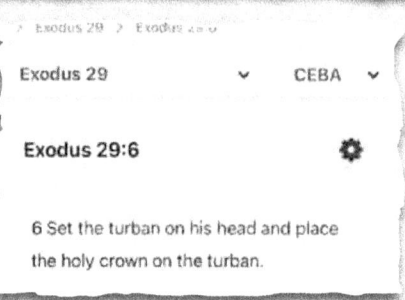

I think this is the one you are looking for though.. Short and to the point.. Cause if Moorish Pendent = Holy Crown then???

Ezekiel 24:17 HCSB
Parallel Verse

Parallel Verses

Holman Bible
Groan quietly; do not observe mourning rites for the dead. Put on your turban and strap your sandals on your feet; do not cover your mustache or eat the bread of mourners."

New American Standard Bible
Groan silently; make no mourning for the dead. Bind on your turban and put your shoes on your feet, and do not cover your mustache and do not eat the bread of men."

One for the Noble Drew Ali Mustache heathens

Exodus 29 — CEBA

Exodus 29:6

6 Set the turban on his head and place the holy crown on the turban.

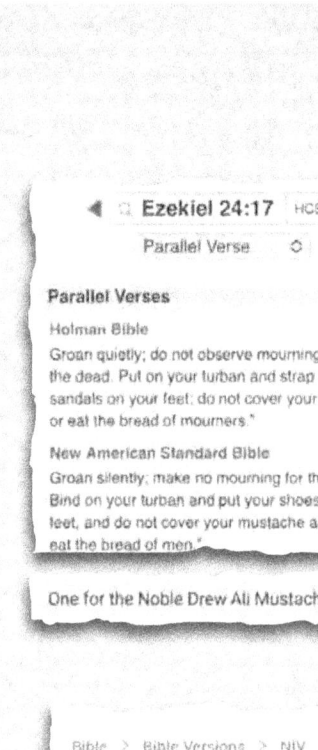

Bible > Bible Versions > NIV > Ezekiel > Ezekiel 44 > Ezekiel 44:18

Ezekiel 44:18

18 They are to wear linen turbans on their heads and linen undergarments around their waists. They must not wear anything that makes them perspire.

Zechariah 3:5 ALL

head. And they set the pure turban upon his head, and clothed him with garments: and the Angel of Jehovah stood by.

Julia Smith Translation
And saying, They shall set a pure turban upon his head; and they will set the pure turban upon his head, and they will put on the garments. And the messenger of Jehovah stood.

King James 2000
And I said, Let them set a clean turban upon his head. So they set a clean turban upon his head, and clothed him with garments. And the angel of the LORD stood by.

Lexham Expanded Bible
And I said, "Let them put a clean headband on his head." And they put a clean headband on his head, and they clothed him [with] garments. And the angel of Yahweh [was] standing [by].

Another Clean and pure nation reference

That what I could find Noble. I Hope that Helps.. Islam

Clean & Pure Nation

What's Really Goin on Here??
Last Ali of the Shariffian Empire.. They gave him the name "Sharif" when he went to the 2nd Kemet.

Aka "The Holy Lands" Hence Holy Crown!!!

gratitude to
Bro. G.S. Aatazaz Bey & Bro. Aseer El

The feather as the symbol is synonymous with Maat and the day of judgement. I'm the America's it was seen as a symbol of the sun rays of the feathered serpent. When the feather is worn with worn with a diadem it's a symbol of the activated pineal organ. Worn ancestral by the high priests of Anu. That's why you only see it worn by Moors. The pale Arabs never wore jewels etc because they were all broke. It's also a customary regalia worn by the Moors before the advent of the "religion" of Islam brought by the Romans and pale Arabs, to thwart the

This is what Aseer told me about the prophets turban

Chapter 6

Wrapping the Moorish Turban

Excerpt from *Hold Me Up: Noble Drew Ali's Lessons on Law & Spirituality*[1]

Noble Drew Ali brought us the turban so we can crown ourselves as people of Universal Consciousness who sit on the throne of commitment to our own higher Self realization and activation. Wrapping the turban is a spiritual practice like wrapping a mummy or wrapping copper around crystals, where we take the highest, most visible part of ourselves—our head—and show that it belongs to the Creator. Wearing the turban also helps cultivate a sense of surrender to the Divine because, depending on the length of the cloth used, this can turn into a very intense meditation. The turban becomes a flag of the Moorish American consciousness as well as a crown of spiritual esoteric divine royalty.

The feather symbolizes truth; that which must rise, also of lightness, dryness, the heavens, height, speed, spaciousness, and flight to the other realm. The expression "a feather in your cap" is used to mean honor to you; it refers to the custom among many cultures of adding a feather in the hat after an achievement. Ostrich feathers mean distinction. A feathered helmet is a triumph. Wearing feathers helps the Moor take on the powers of the birds, including transcendence, instinctual knowledge, and flight. Feathers are omens of light burdens and even of attainment of goals.

The history of the Turban

The history of the turban is vast. Its wearing goes back to ancient Moabite days, when the turban was worn by Moabite women as an honour to their crown. It signified that she was the personification of divinity, because she wrapped her crown chakra to guard this spiritual seat from infiltration by outside influencing forces.

The word "turban" comes from the old Persian word "dhulban" (pronounced "thool-ban"). The word "dhulban" means "rose petal". This word was chosen for the "head wrap" because the folds of the turban resemble the petals of a rose.

The rose is also an emblem representing secrecy. The ancient Moabite word for the turban is "immah". The ancient Moabite/Arabic word "immah", comes from the word "ummi" or "um" (pronounced "oom"), meaning "mother". So, either way you look at it the turban is related to the woman.

The Moabite/Moorish men wear the turban as ADEPTS in the Ancient Mysteries, which ALL were describing the divinity of the Moorish woman. Thus, when we ascend to the 3rd heaven, we find the pass-

The Moorish Turban[2]

A.C. / M.S.T.A. 24

The Turban is not only worn as a casual headdress, it is also worn as a HOLY CROWN, as evidenced by the PROPHET in his most ancient royal garb. The headdress is worn universally by Moslems throughout the Asiatic Nations of the Earth Land.

THE TURBAN represents the CIRCLE of which is 360 degrees. Just as the Moorish Fez, this wrapping or crowing of the head is the sealing of the forehead by the Head, Chief Angel.

Most times the Turban is wrapped **right over left** and when done this way, it represents higher self over lower self, right over wrong, etc.

When wrapped **left over right** it represents the seen and the unseen; with the left side (seen) representing the flesh, and the right side in this case represents the unseen spirits of ALLAH. The Moorish American of today prefer the mentioned (right over left).

The colors of the Moorish Turban are very significant as the Prophet said that we Moors could wear the colors of the rainbow. Therefore, the representations of the colors come in, with the basic colors being RED, GREEN, and BLUE. The RED as we know represents

DIVINE LOVE/ BLOOD; GREEN represents NOURISHMENT/ EARTH and FERTILITY; BLUE represents ROYALTY. GOLD represents the HEALING POWERS of EARTH; PURPLE represents THE RULER, and WHITE, of course, represents PURITY; BLACK represents DEATH and worn by the adept as they are those who have attained unto a measure of faith; the adept has gained enough faith to be firmly rooted in Drew Ali, thus escaping death of which is the state that the Prophet found us. Colors such as BROWN, BEIGE, TAN, etc., are tones of THE EARTH LAND in tune with NATURE. The color YELLOW represents EXTREME CAUTION and is sometimes used to represent COWARDICE.

The Moorish turban is wrapped with a strip or two; the strip of cloth represents THE CORD that stretches from THE HEART OF MAN to the HEART OF ALLAH. This is the reason why we don't let the cords hang past our chest area, down to the area of the private parts; as we don't want to draw energy from these parts of the body, but only from the height of our frames. A woman is not restricted to, but usually wraps the turban with strips (cords) around her shoulders.

...the turban represents wisdom—the wisdom that speaks from the highest planes of spirit life. We know that this is the Motherly or feminine aspect of ALLAH. Woman is part of life or creation, and represents the WISDOM OF ALLAH; THE STILL SMALL VOICE, HOLY BREATH, ETC.

"The turban, which to many is the distinguishing feature of an Oriental costume, though by no means so universal as is generally inferred, is in Morocco almost always white, the size corresponding to the wearer's idea of his own importance."[3]

How to Wrap the Moorish Turban

Sister Noble Sunny Bell Bey of EmpressedTurbans.com generously provides visual instruction on how to wrap the turban traditionally worn by Moorish Americans.

*Images have been reversed to match what you would see while wrapping in a mirror.

Sis. Sunny Bey is shown in a 72" wrap from her line of turbans at EmpressedTurbans.com

How Much Cloth Should I Use?

From Rahs Bey

108" x 18" or 27", or 36" wide.
Depends on cloth texture. Stays 108 (length). But if thin will need 36" wide. If thicker like stretch material, can be 27".
Measurements come out to divine "9".

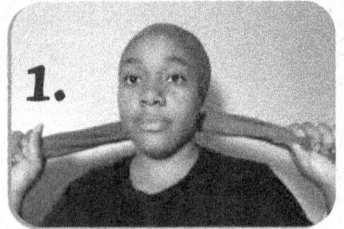 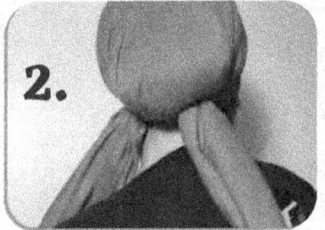  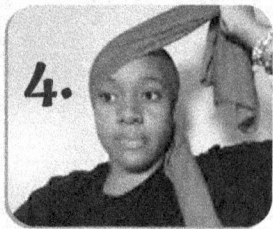

1. Begin by wrapping cloth smoothly over the head, and evenly across the forehead. If the fabric is not hemmed, fold a portion under to create a straight edge before wrapping. Gather ends into tails with the left side being shorter than the right.
2. Cross or tie tails at the nape of the neck securing dome section at cross point. Now the right side will be shorter than the left.
3. Grasp cloth in the left hand and ensure edges are straight.
4. Pull cloth diagonally across the forehead hem to the right side of the head. Smooth cloth as you go.

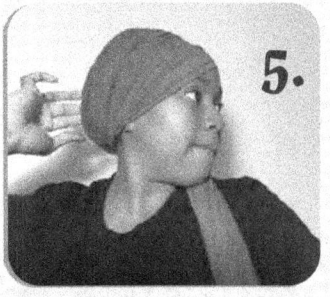  

5. Continue to wrap until reaching the end of the fabric tail.
6. Tuck tail end into fold.
7. Take right side of fabric and pull diagonally across the forehead to the left side of the head.
8. Adjust fabric to form the peak of the turban as you go.
9. Wrap around to the back of the head until the end of the tail is reached.
10. Tuck end of tail into fold.

  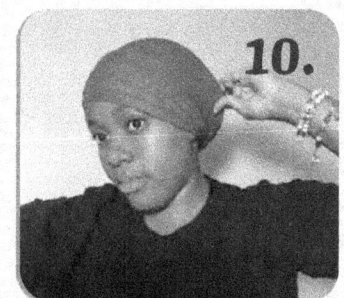

Done.

Sisters are encouraged to place the Moorish American button at the peak in the middle of the forehead where the two sides of the fabric cross.

How to Wrap the Turban w/ Halo

Another variation of the Moslem turban where two wraps are used to create a halo twist. Visit Sis. Sunny at EmpressedTurbans.com for more wrapping options.

Images have been reversed to match what you would see when wrapping in a mirror.

Materials
- *Two short turban (72"): Color A (for halo) // Color B (main turban)*

1. Beginning with the halo turban (Color A/ green), start wrapping as you would for a traditional turban, stopping before crossing the tails of the fabric across the forehead.
2. Take the main turban (Color B/ pink) and
3. drape it over the head, again, as if wrapping a traditional turban.
4. Tie the tails of Color B, pulling both tails of Color A through the knot before tying.
5. Bring both tails of Color A to the front and let the lay across your right shoulder.

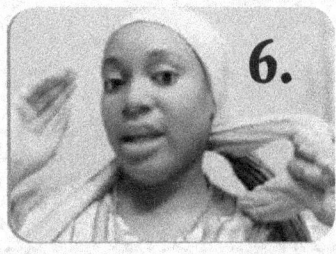  

6. Pull the RIGHT tail of Color B under the two tails of Color A.
7. The knotted tails of Color B should be tied around the hanging tails of Color A.
8-9. Continue to wrap turban Color B using the traditional wrapping instructions.
10. You now have a wrapped turban with two tails hanging over your right shoulder.

11. Smooth the two tails of Color A and begin evenly twisting them together to the end of the tails. Twist the ends into one another so they can be neatly tucked in.
12. Wrap the halo twist across the forehead to the back to the head and tuck in ends.
13. DONE.

How to Wrap the Saracen's Turban

Jamhal Talib Abdullah Bey demonstrates wrapping the turban of the Saracen; the heroic warrior able to cross all seas—be they water or sand—immediately recognizable by the distinctive *litham* that can be used to conceal toe wearer's facial expressions or guard from aerial pollutants. This style requires

*Images have been reversed to match what you would see while wrapping in a mirror.

Materials
- *Satin or silk under-cap/beanie*
- *One short turban (72")*
- *One long turban (108")*

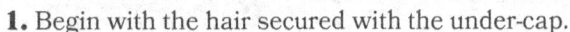

1. Begin with the hair secured with the under-cap.
2. Drape the long turban (gray) evenly over the head with hem level across the forehead.
3. - 4. Wrap the short turban (red) twice around the head as shown—it may be wrapped right-to-left or left-to-right as preferred (see *page 88*). The forehead hem of the long turban should be under the wrapped long turban. Adjust as needed so that the under-cap is visible beneath the short turban.

5. Take the right side tail of the long turban and pull it up and over diagonally across to the left side of the head, back around to the center of the forehead

6. 7. Here, carefully twist the fabric, then pull it downward and diagonally to the left, under the ear, and back around to the center of the forehead.

8. Wrap in this way until the end of the tail is reached, then tuck into fabric to secure.

9. Take the remaining left tail of the long turban and, going from left to right, wrap it loosely around the back of the head so that it drapes cover the back of the neck.

10. Tuck one corner of the tail into the wrapped part of the turban and you are done.

Endnotes

1. Kudjo Adwo El, "National Headdress," in *Hold Me up: Noble Drew Ali's Lessons on Law & Spirituality*, ed. Tauheedah Najee-Ullah El (Lafayette, IN: Califa Media Publishing, 2021), pp. 60-64.
2. Ibid.
3. Budgett Meakin, "How the Moors Dress," in *The Moors: A Comprehensive Description* (London, 1906), 58.

References

Memorandum and Introduction

Noble Drew Ali, Timothy. "Koran Questions for Moorish Americans: 101s and Additional Laws." Essay. In *Califa Uhuru: A Compliation of Literature from the Moorish Science Temple of America* 4, edited by Tauheedah Najee-Ullah El, 4:138–48. Califa Uhuru. Lafayette, Indiana: Califa Media Publishing, 2014.

"Pictographic." The Free Dictionary. Farlex. Accessed August 20, 2022. https://www.thefreedictionary.com/pictographic.

"What Is a 'Chronicle'?" Chronicle. Accessed August 20, 2022. https://www.onechronicle.com/help/.

Chapter 1: Defining the Turban

Clifford, Garth C. "Feather Symbolism & Meaning (+Totem, Spirit & Omens)." World Birds, September 24, 2021. https://worldbirds.com/feather-symbolism/#colors.

Cohn, Bernard S. *Colonialism and Its Forms of Knowledge the British in India*. Princeton, NJ: Princeton University Press, 1996. 116

Consuelo. "La Toca, Turbantes (Y Ii)." LA TOCA, Turbantes (y II), January 1, 1970. https://opusincertumhispanicus.blogspot.com/2013/02/la-toca-y-2.html.

Dennis, Tiara. "Rose Symbolism: New Beginning and Hope." Sun Signs, July 14, 2021. https://www.sunsigns.org/rose-symbolism-meanings/.

"Feather Meaning and Spiritual Symbolism: The Ultimate Guide." A Little Spark of Joy, May 8, 2022. https://www.alittlesparkofjoy.com/feather-meaning/.

"Flag of Luxembourg." Encyclopædia Britannica. Encyclopædia Britannica, inc. Accessed October 19, 2022. https://www.britannica.com/topic/flag-of-Luxembourg.

Holaday, Carol. *Crafting a Magical Life: Manifesting Your Heart's Desire Through Creative Projects*. Forres, Scottland: Findhorn Press, 2009.

"The Jewellery Editor." www.thejewelleryeditor.com. Accessed November 21, 2022. https://www.thejewelleryeditor.com/images/a-navratna-turban-with-its-sacred-combination-of-nine-gemstones-by-c-krishniah-chetty-and-sons/.

Judge, Lindsay. "Your Comprehensive History of a Turban." A&E Magazine, November 23, 2018. https://aeworld.com/fashion/fashion-women/your-comprehensive-history-of-a-turban/.

Mahfuz El Bey, Mishaal Talib. *The Torch: A Guide to S.E.L.F.* Lafayette, Indiana: Califa Media Publishing, 2020. 461

MS, Abhilash. "Traditional Settings of Navaratna Gems." Traditional Settings of Navaratna Gems. Hindu Devotional Blog, July 6, 2021. https://www.hindudevotionalblog.com/2011/12/traditional-settings-of-navaratna-gems.html.

Nicolle, David, and Angus McBride. Essay. In *The Moors: The Islamic West 7th-15th Century AD*, 44–45. Oxford: Osprey Military, 2008.

Pedia, Team Utsav. "Turban or Pagri: The Pride of Marwar." Utsavpedia, May 2, 2017. https://www.utsavpedia.com/attires/pagri-the-pride-of-marwar/.

Pokazanyeva Foxen, Anya. "Turbans, Certain to Charm! South Asian Men, White Women, and the Gendering of Early American Yoga." Interdisciplinary Humanities Center UCSB, May 22, 2017. https://ihc.ucsb.edu/turbans-certain-to-charm/.

Richardson, Connor H. "The Coverings of an Empire: An Examination of Ottoman Headgear from 1500 to 1829." The Cupola: Scholarship at Gettysburg College, 2012. https://cupola.gettysburg.edu/student_scholarship/104.

Sheard, K. M. *Llewellyn's Complete Book of Names: For Pagans, Witches, Wiccans, Druids, Heathens, Mages, Shamans and Independent Thinkers of All Sorts Who Are Curious About Names from Every Place and Every Time*. Minneapolis, MN: Llewellyn, 2012.

Sheridan, Patricia. "Time of the Turban: Headgear Has Different Meanings for Different Cultures." GoSanAngelo. Pittsburgh Post-Gazette, January 23, 2015. https://archive.gosanangelo.com/lifestyle/time-of-the-turban-headgear-has-different-meanings-for-different-cultures-ep-894427809-353655661.html/.

Sikh Dharma International & filed under Bana. "The Spiritual Technology of the Turban." Sikh Dharma International, March 28, 2018. https://www.sikhdharma.org/the-spiritual-technology-of-the-turban/.

Singh, Neutral. "Heritage of the Turban." Sikh Philosophy Network. Sikh Philosophy Network, August 2, 2004. https://www.sikhphilosophy.net/threads/heritage-of-the-turban.440/.

"The Spiritual Meaning & Symbolism of Feathers." YourTango, July 4, 2022. https://wwwyourtango.com/2020337386/feather-meanings-spiritual-meaning-symbolism-feathers.

Stewart, Courtney A. "In the Stars: Gems and the Indian Tradition." Metmuseum.org, December 17, 2014. https://www.metmuseum.org/blogs/now-at-the-met/2014/in-the-stars-gems-and-the-indian-tradition.

Sunny Diamonds. "Everything You Should Know About Navaratna Diamond Jewellery." Sunny Diamonds, June 21, 2021. https://sunnydiamonds.com/blog/everything-you-should-know-about-navaratna-diamond-jewellery/.

Tresidder, Jack. "Feather." Essay. In *The Watkins Dictionary of Symbols*. London: Watkins, 2008.

Chapter 2: India

"Dastar." The Reader Wiki, Reader View of Wikipedia. Accessed October 22, 2022. https://thereaderwiki.com/en/Dastar. [Image 5, 6]

Wright, Colin. "Jodhpur: Sardar Singh, Maharaja of Jodhpur (1880-1911)." The British Library - The British Library. The British Library, September 12, 2008. https://www.bl.uk/onlinegallery/onlineex/apac/photocoll/j/019pho000000099u00004000.html. [Image 3]

"Muhammad Khan Zaman Khan." Wikipedia Commons. Wikimedia Foundation, July 1, 2022. https://en.wikipedia.org/wiki/Muhammad_Khan_Zaman_Khan. [Image 1]

Rathore, Abhinay. "Pictures from Rajput Provinces of India." Rajput Provinces of India. Accessed November 22, 2022. https://www.indianrajputs.com/pictures.php?category=Portraits&page=30. [Image 4]

"Sir Arjun Singh, Raja of Narsinghgarh (c. 1900)." Wikipedia Commons. Wikipedia Foundation. Accessed November 22, 2022. https://commons.wikimedia.org/wiki/File:Sir_Arjun_Singh,_Raja_of_Narsinghgarh_(c._1900).jpg. [Image 2]

"The Turban That Rocked the RCMP: How Baltej Singh Dhillon Challenged the RCMP - and Won | CBC Canada 2017." CBCnews. CBC/Radio Canada, May 11, 2017. https://www.cbc.ca/2017/canadathestoryofus/the-turban-that-rocked-the-rcmp-how-baltej-singh-dhillon-challenged-the-rcmp-and-won-1.4110271. [Image 8]

"World's Biggest Turban." DangerousMinds, August 4, 2014. https://dangerousminds.net/comments/worlds_biggest_turban. [Image 7]

Chapter 3: Europe

"100% Artisan Moor's Heads - Authentic Caltagirone Ceramics." DD Ceramiche Siciliane. Accessed October 24, 2022. https://ddceramichesiciliane.com/en-us/collections/teste-di-moro. [Image 38]

"20th Century, Possibly by Nardi." A GOLD, DIAMOND AND CORAL FIGURAL BROOCH. Accessed December 24, 2022. https://www.christies.com/lot/lot-a-gold-diamond-and-coral-figural-brooch-6013647/?from=salesummery&intobjectid=6013647&sid=a8ed8460-0301-4572-920f-7d6b66a9e5d9. [Image 42]

"Adoration of the Magi (Stom)." Wikipedia. Wikimedia Foundation, December 9, 2021. https://en.wikipedia.org/wiki/Adoration_of_the_Magi_(Stom). [Image 7]

"Adoration of the Magi (the J. Paul Getty Museum Collection)." Getty. Accessed November 23, 2022. https://www.getty.edu/art/collection/object/103RHD. [Image 4]

"The Adoration of the Magi (the J. Paul Getty Museum Collection)." Getty. Accessed November 23, 2022. https://www.getty.edu/art/collection/object/103RX7. [Image 3]

"Antique Blackamoor 18k Yellow Gold Brooch and Earrings." Cris Notti Jewels, September 18, 2019. https://www.crisnottijewels.com/product/antique-blackamoor-18k-yellow-gold-brooch-earrings/. [Image 41]

"Bashi-Bazouk Ca. 1868–69 Jean-Léon Gérôme French." Metmuseum.org. Accessed October 23, 2022. https://www.metmuseum.org/art/collection/search/651837. [Image 25]

"The Black Africans Who Ruled Europe from 711 to 1789." Nairaland, The Nigerian Forum. Accessed November 23, 2022. https://www.nairaland.com/3721445/black-africans-ruled-europe-711. [Image 10]

Casanova, Giacomo. T*he Memoirs of Jacques Casanova De Seingalt: The Prince of Adventurer*s. 1. Vol. 1. Boston: L.C. Page, 1903. [Image 18]

"Coppia Teste Di Moro." Ceramiche Cannarozzo, April 6, 2021. https://www.ceramichecannarozzo.com/prodotto/coppia-teste-di-moro/. [Image 39]

Costa, Gino. "Venice- Campo Dei Mori (The Champ of the Moors)." Cercodiamanti, January 10, 2015. http://dipoco.altervista.org/venice-campo-dei-mori-champ-moors/?doing_wp_cron=1666492930.1498749256134033203125. [Image 1]

"Giovanni Battista Piazzetta (1682-1754) - An Archer in a Turbanned Headdress." Royal Collection Trust. Accessed October 23, 2022. https://www.rct.uk/collection/990755/an-archer-in-a-turbanned-headdress. [Image 14]

"Jan Gossaert Circle - Adoration of the Kings." File:Jan Gossaert circle - Adoration of the Kings.jpg. Wikimedia Commons. Accessed November 23, 2022. https://commons.wikimedia.org/wiki/File:Jan_Gossaert_001_detail_highres.jpg. [Image 13]

"Jan Van Bijlert: Caspar (1640-1650)." Artsy. Accessed August 22, 2022. https://www.artsy.net/artwork/jan-van-bijlert-caspar. [Image 8]

"Jean Discart - The Connoisseurs." Wikipedia. Wikimedia Foundation, November 11, 2021. https://en.wikipedia.org/wiki/Jean_Discart. [Image 28]

"Jean-Etienne Liotard." Wikipedia. Wikimedia Foundation, December 8, 2022. https://en.wikipedia.org/wiki/Jean-%C3%89tienne_Liotard. [Image 15b]

"Le Jeune Ottoman." Budapestaukcio.hu. Accessed September 23, 2022. https://budapestaukcio.hu/hans-johan-fredrik-berg/festo/le-jeune-ottoman-5485401. [Image 20]

"Ludwig Deutsch - The Inspection 1883." Sothebys.com. Accessed October 23, 2022. https://www.sothebys.com/en/auctions/ecatalogue/2010/19th-century-european-art-n08673/lot.7.html. [Image 27]

"Ludwig Deutsch - The Treasure Chest, 1920.JPG." Wikimedia.org. Wikimedia Foundation. Accessed October 24, 2022. https://commons.wikimedia.org/wiki/File:Ludwig_Deutsch_-_The_Treasure_Chest,_1920.jpg. [Image 30}

"Man in Oriental Costume." Art Object Page. Accessed November 23, 2022. https://www.nga.gov/collection/art-object-page.572.html. [Image 6]

"A Man Wearing a Turban and Armour - Karel Van Mander III." USEUM. Accessed November 23, 2022. https://useum.org/artwork/A-Man-Wearing-a-Turban-and-Armour-Karel-van-Mander-III-1647. [Image 9]

"Marie José Jean Raymond Silbert - Type Marocain (1905) ." Mutual Art. Accessed October 24, 2022. https://www.mutualart.com/Artwork/Type-Marocain/030F8A66B0FB6FA0. [Image 29]

"Moor Woman Head with Striped Blue and Green Turban Vase." Artemest. Accessed November 24, 2022. https://artemest.com/products/moor-head-with-striped-blue-and-green-turban-vase. [Image 33]

"Moorish Head De Bellis Dec.. Turquoise." Ceramiche d'Arte – Ravello. Accessed October 24, 2022. https://www.ceramichedarte.com/product/moors-head-de-bellis-dec-turquoise/. [Image 35]

"Moorish Head De Bellis Dec.. Turquoise." Ceramiche d'Arte – Ravello. Accessed October 24, 2022. https://www.ceramichedarte.com/product/moors-head-de-bellis-dec-turquoise/. [Image 37]

"Moorish Man with Turban in Half-Length Attributed to Jan Lievens." PubHist. Accessed October 23, 2022. https://www.pubhist.com/w6020. [Image 5]

The National Gallery. "Jan Van Eyck, Portrait of a Man (Self Portrait?)." Jan van Eyck | Portrait of a Man (Self Portrait?) | NG222. National Gallery, London, January 1, 1970. https://www.nationalgallery.org.uk/paintings/jan-van-eyck-portrait-of-a-man-self-portrait. [Image 2]

"Noma Displays an African Tronie from the Dutch Golden Age." New Orleans Museum of Art, April 22, 2020. https://noma.org/noma-acquires-an-african-tronie-from-the-dutch-golden-age/. [Image 11]

"The Orange Seller." The Black Art Depot. Accessed October 23, 2022. https://www.blackartdepot.com/products/the-orange-seller-ludwig-deutsch. [Image 19]

"Orientalist Oil on Canvas Moorish Princess." LiveAuctioneers. Accessed September 23, 2022. https://www.liveauctioneers.com/item/79597244_orientalist-oil-on-canvas-moorish-princess. [Image 22]

"A Pair of Tortoiseshell Inlaid Premtalian Gilt-Bronze-Mounted Marble Busts of Blackamoors... Stamped N. P. Severin, Régence, circa 1715." Sothebys.com. Accessed November 23, 2022. https://www.sothebys.com/en/auctions/ecatalogue/2010/treasures-aristocratic-heirlooms-l10307/lot.6.html. [Image 12]

"Portrait of a Moorish Servant, Full-Length, in Classical Hunting Dress and a Turban, with a Couple of Hounds." Circle of Jonathan Richardson, Sen. (1665-1745). Accessed November 23, 2022. https://www.christies.com/en/lot/lot-4825593. [Image 21]

"Portrait of a Young Woman." Saint Louis Art Museum, December 2, 2022. https://www.slam.org/collection/objects/20200/. [Image 15a]

"Rare Artwork from the Orientalist Stable." The difference between a Moroccan and a Zanzibari Nimcha. - ethnographic arms & armour, September 16, 2016. http://www.vikingsword.com/vb/showthread.php?t=21833&highlight=NIMCHA. [Image 24]

Röell Guus. "5. Portrait of a Black African Boy." Essay. In *Uit Verre Streken: Luxury Goods from Dutch Trading Posts in the West Indies, East Indies, China, Japan and Africa, 17th-19th Centuries*, 10–11. Maastricht: Guus Röell, 2018.

"Sicilian Ceramic 'Moor's Head' from Caltagirone, Sicilian Ceramic. Decor White Line Gender Woman Type Turban Modello Vaso Height 30 Cm." Sofia Ceramiche snc - Teste di Moro. Accessed October 24, 2022. https://www.testedimoro.com/en/moor-s-heads/772-testa-h-30-nacre-donna-modern-moorish-heads-sofia-ceramiche.html. [Image 36]

"Sir John Everett Millais a Moorish Chief Engraving Signed." Lot Art. Accessed October 23, 2022. https://www.lot-art.com/auction-lots/Sir-John-Everett-Millais-A-Moorish-Chief-engraving-signed/183-sir_john-04.9.22-kcm. [Image 26]

"Sold at Auction 18kt Gold Gem-Set Blackamoor Brooch, Nardi Auction Number 2693b Lot Number 394: Skinner Auctioneers." Skinner Inc. Accessed October 24, 2022. https://www.skinnerinc.com/auctions/2693B/lots/394. [Image 40]

Study of a Boy. Art UK. Accessed September 23, 2022. https://artuk.org/discover/artworks/study-of-a-boy-7956. [Image 16]

Tate. "'Christiaan Van Molhoop', Ozias Humphry, C.1795." Tate. Tate Museum, December 31, 1794. https://www.tate.org.uk/art/artworks/humphry-christiaan-van-molhoop-t13796. [Image 17]

"Teste Di Moro 100% Artigianali - Ceramiche Di Caltagirone Autentiche." DD Ceramiche Siciliane. Accessed November 24, 2022. https://en.ddceramichesiciliane.com/collections/teste-di-moro. [Image 34]

TITLE: *"The Abduction of Rebecca by a Knight Templar."* Photograph. *Instagram.com.* @i.i.mcdxcii, March 5, 2022. https://www.instagram.com/i.i.mcdxcii/.

Weeks, Emily M. "Ludwig Deutsch (Austrian, 1855-1935) the Goza Smoker." Bonhams. Accessed October 24, 2022. https://www.bonhams.com/auction/25444/lot/65/ludwig-deutsch-austrian-1855-1935-the-goza-smoker/. [Image31]

"William Derby - 'The Fruit Bearer', Oil on Panel, Signed and Dated 1844 Recto, Titled Gall." Toovey's, Fine Art & Antique Auctioneers & Valuers in Sussex. Accessed October 23, 2022. https://www.tooveys.com/lots/403073/william-derby-the-fruit-bearer/. [Image 23]

Chapter 4: Africa America

Adwo El, Kudjo. "National Headdress." Essay. In Hold Me up: Noble Drew Ali's Lessons on Law & Spirituality, edited by Tauheedah Najee-Ullah El, 60–64. Lafayette, IN: Califa Media Publishing, 2021. [Image 3]

"Agostino Brunias - Free Women of Color with Their Children and Servants in a Landscape." Wikipedia. Wikimedia Foundation, December 12, 2022. https://en.wikipedia.org/wiki/Agostino_Brunias#/media/File:Agostino_Brunias_-_Free_Women_of_Color_with_their_Children_and_Servants_in_a_Landscape_-_Google_Art_Project.jpg. [Image 3]

"Al-Rashid of Morocco." Wikipedia. Wikimedia Foundation, December 20, 2022. https://en.wikipedia.org/wiki/Al-Rashid_of_Morocco#/media/File:Mulay_al-Rashid.jpg.

"Aunt Jemima and Uncle Mose Salt and Pepper Shakers - Nov 21, 2009: Mosby & Co.. Auctions in MD." LiveAuctioneers. Accessed November 26, 2022. https://www.liveauctioneers.com/item/6820686_338-aunt-jemima-and-uncle-mose-salt-and-pepper-shakers. [Image 10]

Ben Levy, Sholomo. "Biography of Rabbi Arnold Josiah Ford." blackjews.org, February 24, 2016. https://www.blackjews.org/biography-of-rabbi-arnold-josiah-ford/. [Image 13]

Blevins, Joe. "The Greatest Pretender: Korla Pandit, Music's Most Magnificent Fraud." Dead 2 Rights. Accessed November 26, 2022. https://d2rights.blogspot.com/2013/05/the-greatest-pretender-korla-pandit.html. [Image 12]

Callender, Samantha. "The Tignon Laws Set the Precedent for the Appropriation and Misconception around Black Hair." Essence. Essence, October 24, 2020. https://www.essence.com/hair/tignon-laws-cultural-appropriation-black-natural-hair/.

"Dido Belle." Scone Palace. Accessed October 25, 2022. https://www.scone-palace.co.uk/dido-belle. [Image 4]

Dorman, Jarnell. "Tignon Law: The Attempted Oppression of African Beauty." ecoterie beauty. ecoterie beauty, September 26, 2020. https://www.ecoteriebeauty.co/blog/tignonlaw.

Gubele, Rose. "Utalotsa Woni—'Talking Leaves': A Re-Examination of the Cherokee Syllabary and Sequoyah." *Studies in American Indian Literatures* 24, no. 4 (2012): 47. https://doi.org/10.5250/studamerindilite.24.4.0047. 58-59

Harris, Karen. "Tignon Laws Forced Black Women to Cover Their Hair." History Daily, July 25, 2020. https://historydaily.org/tignon-laws-facts-trivia-stories.

"Korla Pandit Discography." Korla Pandit Official Site. Accessed November 26, 2022. http://www.korlapandit.com/discography.htm.

"NPS Ethnography: African American Heritage & Ethnography." National Parks Service. U.S. Department of the Interior. Accessed October 18, 2022. https://www.nps.gov/ethnography/aah/aaheritage/lowCountryc.htm.

Parkins, H. "Aunt Jemima, What Took You so Long?" National Archives and Records Administration. National Archives and Records Administration. Accessed October 18, 2022. https://prologue.blogs.archives.gov/2011/08/03/aunt-jemima-what-took-you-so-long/. [Image 9]

Pilgram, David. "The Mammy Caricature." Ferris State University, October 2000. https://www.ferris.edu/HTMLS/news/jimcrow/mammies/homepage.htm. [Image 8]

"Priestly Turban." Wikipedia. Wikimedia Foundation, May 12, 2022. https://en.wikipedia.org/wiki/Priestly_turban.

"Sequoyah, Cherokee Inventor, by C.B. King, 1836.JPG." Wikimedia. Wikimedia Foundation. Accessed November 29, 2022. https://commons.wikimedia.org/wiki/File:Sequoyah,_Cherokee_inventor,_by_C.B._King,_1836.jpg. [Image 5]

"Slavery and the Making of America . the Slave Experience: Men, Women & Gender: PBS." Slavery and the Making of America . The Slave Experience: Men, Women & Gender | PBS. Accessed October 26, 2022. https://www.thirteen.org/wnet/slavery/experience/gender/feature6.html. [Image 6, 7]

"Tribal Lifestyle: The Life of the Tuareg." Ootlah, November 2, 2021. https://www.ootlah.com/en/blog/tribal-lifestyle-life-tuareg.html. [Image 1]

Who Got Paid to Help Keep Slaves? Colonial Indictments & Another #MessedUpMoorishStory . Califa Media Publishing, 2022. https://youtu.be/KPsgnzYTeYA.